BL859Te

Teague.

   Mrs L: conversations with Alice
Roosevelt Longworth.

1981

Alice Roosevelt in 1902 by Theobald Chartran

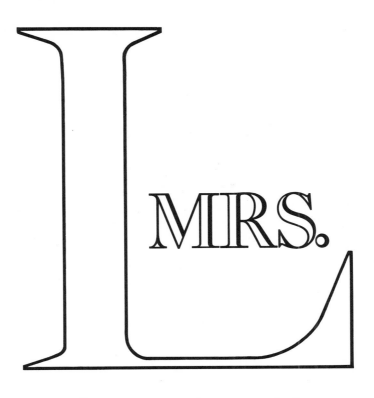

MRS. L

Conversations with
Alice Roosevelt Longworth

Michael Teague

Doubleday & Company, Inc.
Garden City, New York
1981

For Joanna

The text on pages 84–108 originally appeared in *Vogue* magazine entitled "Alice in Plunderland." Courtesy VOGUE. Copyright © 1972 by the Condé Nast Publications, Inc.

(*Cont'd. on page 203*)

Library of Congress Cataloging in Publication Data
Longworth, Alice Roosevelt, 1884–1980
Mrs. L: conversations with Alice Roosevelt Longworth.

1. Longworth, Alice Roosevelt, 1884–1980. 2. Politicians'
wives—United States—Biography. 3. Presidents
—United States—Children—Biography. I. Teague,
Michael. II. Title.
E748.L87L83   973.9'092'4 [B]
ISBN *0-385-13382-0*
Library of Congress Catalog Card Number 78–22360
Copyright © 1981 by Michael Teague

Acknowledgments

I would like to thank the following for the help they have given in the preparation of this book:

Sylvia and Edmund Morris for their careful review of the manuscript and for their many useful suggestions; Letitia Bonbright, who first started the tapes running with Mrs. Longworth; Kay Halle, Kristie Twadell, Eric W. Alderfer, Susan-Mary Alsop, Gary Kisner, Lynn Magruder, David Lee, Janie McLaughlin, Bob Hamilton, Monie Begley, Kurt Ross, Ginette Spanier, Robert Hellman, Dorothy and Henry Breck, Alexandra Roosevelt, Claudette Colbert, Leroy Woodson; Frances Schuchard and June Irish for their careful typing of the manuscript; and my sister, Zélide Cowan, for her many helpful ideas about its presentation.

Dr. John Gable, the Director of the Theodore Roosevelt Association, and Mr. Wallace Dailey, the Curator of the Theodore Roosevelt Collection at Harvard, gave me invaluable assistance, as did Mr. Jerry Kearns of the Library of Congress and Mr. Gary Roth, the Curator at Sagamore Hill National Historic Site.

My thanks also go to Robin Breckenridge for the help she gave with the layout and jacket design, and to my editor at Doubleday, Carolyn Blakemore, her assistant James Moser, Alex Gotfryd, the Art Director, and Larry Alexander for all the trouble they took over the presentation of the book.

Above all, my greatest debt of gratitude goes to Mrs. Longworth herself, without whose cooperation this book would obviously never have been written, and to her granddaughter, Joanna Sturm, the silent partner in what she called "a play about a play."

Introduction

I first bumped into Alice Roosevelt Longworth—"Mrs. L." as she was usually known to her friends—shortly after coming to Washington in 1961. The car I was in stopped too late at a traffic light and collided gently with her very ancient Cadillac. The chauffeur, who appeared to be the same vintage as the car, turned around to check what had happened, but the figure sitting in the center of the back seat never moved. Her large, flat black hat seemed to float calmly just above the top of the seat. I think she was reading.

When I saw her again it was at a luncheon given by mutual friends. As she hardly ever got up before two in the afternoon, they must have been privileged. I remember the quick way she entered the room. There was a vital quality about her that was almost electric in its impact. She walked rapidly and effortlessly with her back and shoulders very straight, a legacy, she claimed, of fighting polio as a child and not wanting to be labeled a cripple. Her movements certainly belied her age. I was later to discover that she was quite capable of sinking gracefully into the lotus position when she was well into her nineties. She could also touch her nose with her big toe without bending forward an inch. It was an incredible sight.

I remember we got into an animated discussion about Franklin Roosevelt's Delano relations at that first meeting. I had acquired a half model of the clipper ship *Memnon*, which had been built for Warren Delano, Franklin Roosevelt's maternal grandfather, and I was telling her about my researches into the family's connection with the China trade. "Do let me know if you discover whether they had any dealings with the opium trade," she said with glee, "because, you see, that would make Franklin a *criminal*." It was my first experience of the conversational leaps she could make. As a young friend of hers once remarked, "Mrs. Longworth has this fantastic imagination. She keeps her mind loose. She listens and follows *your* associations. The conversation doesn't move in a straight line. You take these giant steps. Almost like someone flipping out on drugs." When this was reported back to her, Mrs. L. said, "That's too much fun! Do you suppose that when I outgrew my hormones I started manufacturing LSD?"[*1]

When I next saw her I took a photograph I had found of a magnificent-looking Japanese gentleman c. 1900 dressed in a gold-embroidered frock coat. She was delighted because it turned out to be an old friend, Count Nagasaki, who had been one of her official hosts when she went to Japan in 1905. That started such a delightful stream of reminiscences about her Far Eastern trip that I asked if I could tape-record them. The results were published in *Vogue* under the title of "Alice in Plunderland." She liked the piece so much that we continued taping, usually at teatime in her house, for the next six years.

These sessions were not interviews in the accepted sense of the word. It was impossible to put rigid structures around anything so mercurial as her talk. Her verbal dexterity was best expressed in the natural flow of conversation rather than in any set pattern of question and answer.

She was an extremely good listener as well and she could draw you out with remarkable skill. "Go on!" and "Tell!" were two of her favorite admonitions. She encouraged excesses. She was never competitive, applauding when others shone, in however modest a way. Of course there was always the danger of being jeered at when you did not—but at least you were *noticed*. "I love the way you bring out the worst in me," one friend told her admiringly.

What I remember most vividly about our teatime sessions was the shared laughter. The tapes are awash with it and the sound of our hilarity frequently drowned the conversation. Her own laugh was distinctive, as was her voice with its occasional deep resonance and wonderful range of intonations. In contrast to what she called her "bark," she said of her granddaughter Joanna's laugh that it was "one of the pleasantest sounds I've ever heard."

Joanna, who had come to live with her at the age of ten, often joined us at teatime. She and her grandmother were very good friends, and they had a healthy respect for each other's independence and idiosyncrasies. I remember Joanna once asking about a close friendship Mrs. L. had with a politician in the twenties. There was a pause, and then:

Mrs. L.: "What do you want? Revelations? With the tape on?

* Notes appear on pages 201–2.

venerable armchair was notorious for not letting you out of it once you were in. Another had a maverick spring that attacked you in improbable places at improbable times. Jostling for "safe" seats around the tea table often became a variation of "musical chairs."

Wherever you sat there was a wealth of fascinating objects to contemplate. On one wall hung a huge Flemish tapestry, which had once been in the White House. There was a grand piano laden with old albums and sheet music and exotic bits of memorabilia. The famous velvet cushion with the embroidered maxim, "If you haven't got any-thing good to say about anyone come and sit by me," perched in the center of the chintz-covered sofa in the corner.

There were pictures everywhere: dark landscapes from the Long-worths' Cincinnati house, a radiant Sargent watercolor of the White House, a Batchelor cartoon of Eleanor and Franklin entitled, "All this . . . and Truman too" ("I keep it in the interest of good clean fun and bad family feelings"), and a hilarious small picture which Mrs. L. called "The Holy Family of the GOP." It depicted the Infant Eisen-hower cradled in Virgin Mary Robert Taft's lap while Senator Joe McCarthy hovered behind as an unlikely St. Joseph. It was designed, she said, "to infuriate my conservative friends."

Then there were some historic photographs of the Dowager Empress of China, the Emperor of Korea, and the Emperor and Empress of Japan in elaborately carved wooden frames. From a large Chinese scroll in one corner of the room a prowling tiger with bulging eyes glared. Mrs. L. always said it was "the spitting image" of her old friend, Dean Acheson.

The whole place was very comfortable in that old-fashioned, slightly shabby way you rarely find today except perhaps in certain English country houses. The Longworths had bought the house in 1925 and very little had changed since. Mrs. L. was one of those people who managed to impose a distinctive style on their surroundings without in any way appearing to "decorate." Her house was the natural reflection of her personality, and hence its unique character.

The dining room, for instance, which didn't look particularly distinguished by day, could be transformed into the most brilliant of Edwardian settings for dinner parties at night. After one such affair I complimented Mrs. L. on the beauty of her table and the quality of her food, and she said, "I have a horrid suspicion that I have been serving the same food and using the same place settings since I gave my first dinner in May 1906."

She always mixed people well at her parties. In a town that wor-

she had the thinnest bread and butter this side of Mayfair. When the Friends of the Kennedy Center produced a cookbook[3] in 1973, Mrs. L.'s contribution stood out in sharp contrast to its elaborate neighbors. "Take a loaf of good, unsliced bread," she suggested. "Butter with sweet butter. Cut a thin slice with a sharp knife. Repeat."

Her telephone, a large old-fashioned black one kept handily near the sofa, used to ring frequently at teatime because her friends knew they could catch her then. She had a particular way of answering it, leaning right across the sofa until she was almost reclining as she cradled the outsized receiver to her ear.

Many of the ensuing conversations were pure Ruth Draper, and I'm glad I kept the tapes running. Here is a transcript of one such call in which CBS is apparently asking her to do an interview.

Mrs. L.: "Hello, yes. They said you had rung. No not a bit. (*Pause.*) You are going to do *what?* Thirty broadcasts? Starting on Saturday? Every facet of a typical woman's life? Bad, bad. As far as I'm concerned anyway. I suppose you will have Mrs. Mesta and Mrs. Cafritz and more like that? But not me, I'm just an old gray mare. It would bore me to begin with. (*Sighs.*) Very well, go ahead. Go on. (*Pause.*) A life of a woman in one broadcast? A broad perspective? How perfectly idiotic! Go on! Well, it all sounds perfectly lovely and I shall certainly watch it. I like a great many of your people and I must say that these opportunities come to me fairly frequently. But, joking aside, I haven't the faintest intention of doing anything. I think it is great fun and very resourceful of you. Tell them the bad news then. Mr. Cronkite? No, you won't have to tell him. Is Bill Paley still with you? Oh good!

"I tell you who I also like among your people. Mr. Rather. He is *so* good. He's sour about things, which gives me great pleasure. He never says he is at the San Clemente White House. He says he is with the 'presidential party.' And he does things with a barely perceptible sneer which I like. Give him my regards. Thank you and good-bye."

We usually had tea in the drawing room, which was on the first floor of the house, facing Massachusetts Avenue. It was a large L-shaped room, very pleasant and cozy on winter evenings when the curtains were drawn and the lamps switched on. In summer, the heavy swags of wisteria that covered the front of the house, and dangled over the windows, gave the room a cool, mysterious, almost subterranean air.

At tea Mrs. L. usually sat on a wine velvet sofa facing the mantelpiece. The rest of us were grouped toadstool fashion around the tea tray on a variety of chairs and other oddments of furniture. One rather

Well, you are not going to have them, you lovely creature, showing your canine teeth with pleasure."

Joanna: "I'm not on the spot, Grammy. You are."

Mrs. L.: "Well, if you really want to know, I suppose you could say that I was adept at skating on thin ice and playing with fire. Nice image, don't you think?"

And then she changed the subject.

She always responded to personal questions in that way. During the many hours we taped together, she rarely referred to matters of great personal concern, except obliquely. She hardly ever talked about her marriage, for instance, or about her daughter, Paulina, who died in 1957. She talked more about the death of her mother and the effect of her father's subsequent total silence on the subject. But that was about all.

She was quite without self-pity, and what she didn't tolerate in herself she certainly didn't tolerate in others. She was not the best person to take one's troubles to. Unless of course they contained an element of physical disaster, recounted in gory detail. She once told me she craved "an occasional good earthquake." I remember Joan Braden, who was a good friend, bringing a bloody toe for her to view. "Oh *good*," said Mrs. L. with satisfaction as the bandage was unfolded. "Thought you would like it," said Joan, as if presenting a choice objet d'art to a collector.

If you didn't expect her to sympathize with your woes, she could be a great morale booster. Her vitality was contagious. You would arrive for tea, a bit frazzled from the office perhaps, and within a short period of time the magic began to work. I think adrenalin had a lot to do with it. She *made* you shift into higher gear, accelerate and compete in the conversational race. The effect was exhilarating.

The tea helped. Every afternoon at five she provided lots of piping-hot Earl Grey's tea from Jackson's in Piccadilly,[2] served either in Rose Medallion porcelain cups or in tall glasses with silver holders, Russian style. It was kept hot by liberal infusions of boiling water from a large silver kettle, which bubbled noisily over a spirit lamp, often neglected by the hostess when the conversation became particularly animated. The sound of that bubbling kettle combined with the clatter of the cups and the laughter of the guests are among the fondest memories I have of those times.

There was a variety of homemade cakes and cookies at tea and invariably a plate of exquisitely fine bread and butter. She had learned the English trick of buttering the bread *before* slicing it. The result was

shiped success, as a friend once noted, you could also meet failures at Mrs. L.'s. Her ninetieth birthday party was perhaps one of the best she ever gave. It would have taken Proust to record all the nuances. It was at the height of the Watergate crisis and President Nixon was there, along with many of his most passionate critics. The resulting undercurrent of tension gave a curious nervous *éclat* to the occasion.

By the time Mrs. L. held her ninety-second birthday, the pace had begun to slacken. Her memory was not what it was and Joanna provided her grandmother with a hilarious list of admonitions, such as "Don't ask Ford who the President is."

Her house was a never-ending source of interest. There were twenty rooms in all and many were crammed with the most eclectic assortment of objects. The attic alone was a treasure trove of memorabilia and the kitchen and pantry would have delighted the staff of "Upstairs, Downstairs."

I loved the huge pantry next door to the dining room. It had great wooden glass-fronted cabinets as high as the ceiling. There were ornate room indicators for the servants' calls, and complicated fuse boxes that must have predated the First World War.

Janie McLaughlin, who had been in Mrs. L.'s service for almost twenty years, presided over this part of the domain. I can still hear the rumble of the dumbwaiter as it brought Mrs. L.'s dinner up from the kitchen to the pantry, for onward transmission by Janie to the private sitting room on the third floor. This room, which she nicknamed the Collyer room after the famous New York recluses, was made charming by faded chintzes and unusual pictures. Books were piled everywhere, on chairs, on the floor, on the huge sofa, which gradually became lopsided with the weight of them all.

The room also contained a large pink and green doll's house, which she had been given as a child by her maternal grandfather. She used to enjoy playing with it and rearranging its contents, especially in the early hours of the morning when she couldn't sleep. She was a great night prowler. Joanna, catching her at it about three one morning, inquired, "What are you up to, Grammy?" "I'm just checking the camp and kicking the tent pegs," her grandmother replied. She was then well into her nineties and was probably searching for Cat, an aged Siamese, who gave her much pleasure in her last years. "I was destined to end up an old maid with a cat," she once said sardonically.

She did most of her reading at night and was probably one of the best-read women of her own or any age. Her range of interests was extraordinarily wide. The library next to her bedroom contained books on every subject, from biography, philosophy, and history to some of her more esoteric interests, such as geology, astronomy, and zoology. Although she was a woman of no marked religious views, she had as thorough a knowledge of the Bible as the average theologian.

Books were an integral part of her life. From her earliest days they had been a pleasure, a joy, and a consolation. Some of her volumes are so worn with use that they almost fall apart on opening. Her *Oxford Book of English Verse*, for instance, had to be tied together with string to keep it together.

She loved poetry and it was a constant source of delight to her. "I was brought up on doggerel," she once said. From the days of "shouting out the *Nibelungenlied* with glee" as a child she had absorbed a very wide if somewhat eclectic range of poetry, which she could retrieve at will from what she called "the palimpsest of memory." I remember her once quoting a short verse from Vachel Lindsay's *The Congo* that was so full of the feeling of danger and suspense that one could almost hear the throb of jungle drums in the background. On occasion Joanna would recite in unison with her verses such as Hadrian's *Animula vagula, blandula*, which were among her favorites.

She was particularly fond of Hilaire Belloc, Rudyard Kipling, Lord Dunsany, whom she knew well, and her father's protégé Edwin Arlington Robinson.

She liked the sonnet from *Captain Craig* which begins "Carmichael had a kind of joke disease" and ends:

> We always laughed at him, no matter what
> The joke was worth. But when a man's brain dies,
> We are not always glad . . . Poor Carmichael.[4]

She had a particular affinity for frogs and often wore a gold one as a talisman. She liked Hilaire Belloc's:

> No animal will more repay
> A treatment kind and fair
> At least so lonely people say
> Who keep a frog (and, by the way,
> They are extremely rare).[5]

Of all the Kipling verses she knew, she particularly enjoyed this one from *The Jungle Book*:

What of the hunting, hunter bold?
Brother, the watch was long and cold.
What of the quarry ye went to kill?
Brother, he crops in the jungle still.
Where is the power that made your pride?
Brother, it ebbs from my flank and side.
Where is the haste that ye hurry by?
Brother, I go to my lair—to die.[6]

She also very much admired a line from Sir Thomas Browne's *Urne-Buriall V:* "But man is a Noble Animal, splendid in ashes, and pompous in the grave, solemnizing Nativities and Deaths with equal lustre, nor omitting Ceremonies of bravery in the infamy of his nature."[7]

She numbered many writers and poets among her friends and was one of the very few people who regularly visited Ezra Pound when he was in Washington's St. Elizabeth's Hospital. She remembered him sitting in an alcove off the ward wearing "at least three hats piled one on top of another."

Her very real love for the pattern and rhythm of words went far beyond the emotion and ideas which they represented. She enjoyed playing with them, throwing them out, watching them sparkle. As her cousin Joe Alsop once said, "She combines verbal exactitude with a certain fancifulness." I suspect she also used words as a form of defense.

Many of her books are full of scraps of paper, containing elaborate private word games. She enjoyed rearranging the same word in an endless variety of anagrams.

Her humor was subtle and often esoteric. She rarely told jokes and, by her own admission, often didn't understand them when they were told to her, even though she pretended she did and laughed heartily at the punch lines.

Her wit, however, was spontaneous and very distinctive. She never repeated any of her witticisms, even though countless others did. And she took delight in attributing some of her more famous epigrams to others. She had merely given them credence, she maintained. For instance, she claimed the quip about President Coolidge looking "as if he had been weaned on a pickle" was actually said by her dentist, and the one about Thomas Dewey looking "like the bridegroom on the wedding cake" was told to her at a party. Even the classic remark after the birth of her daughter, that "having a baby is like trying to push a grand piano through a transom," she attributed to somebody else. When I asked her about something I *know* she said about General MacArthur and his carefully arranged bald pate ("Never trust a man who combs his hair straight from his left armpit") she scornfully dismissed it, saying, "Oh, that's an old eighteenth-century joke." One of the few quotes she did admit to was the one about Wendell Willkie "springing from the grassroots of the country clubs of America."

I have a feeling that one advantage of not claiming credit for many of these witticisms was that it allowed her to laugh at them much more than she could have otherwise. She certainly didn't consider herself witty. She once said to me, "It's curious how often when one speaks the truth, people say 'How witty!' It's not witty. It's accurate." She maintained that Pope's lines,

> Her wit allured, as obvious as her eyes,
> Less wit than mimic, more wit than wise,

fitted her perfectly.

Although she could be cutting and pricked quite a few balloons in her time, she was not deliberately cruel and she herself was often the butt of her own humor. Anyone who could describe herself after two mastectomies as "the only topless octogenarian in Washington" and, on seeing a rather gnarled picture of herself in her nineties, "I look just like an aging Eurasian concubine," must have had an ability for self-mockery.

Her conversational barbs were swift and direct. She once said about someone that he was "not only a snob, but a stupid snob: snobbish about the wrong people." And after visiting the home of an immensely wealthy but rather ignorant woman, who prided herself on her collection of antique French furniture, Mrs. L. quipped, "She proudly showed me something she claimed was Marie Antoinette's television cabinet."

Her humor had a rather special quality. Take this example which occurred not long before she died. She was eating very little indeed and one night, as she was valiantly trying to "worry-down" her dinner, Joanna said, "Drink up your soup, Grammy. You don't want Harriet [the cook] to quit, do you?" "No, I don't want Harriet to quit," Mrs. L. replied. "I just want her to quit making salmon soup."

One of the problems of trying to recapture the flow of her conversation in writing is that she never spoke in a monologue for any length of time. Her forte was the one-liner, the unfinished sentence, the allusion you were left to puzzle over. Her talk was never predictable, as I found when there had to be some necessary stitching of broken-off conversations for continuity.

In print you miss the eloquence of her facial expressions, her extraordinary timing, and the varied intonations of her voice. I commented on this when I wrote the piece about her trip to the Far East, saying that "it was a pity that one couldn't catch her bubbly quality in print." She was amused by that and when she once signed a picture of herself for me she drew a small self-caricature in the corner with a large balloon saying, "From one who bubbles nicely."

Although a good mimic in private, she was petrified of public speaking. The promotional lectures that coincided with the publication in 1933 of her autobiography, *Crowded Hours*, were agony to her. She quite liked the question and answer period afterward but suffered real stage fright beforehand. President Kennedy once asked her if she wanted to say a few words at the dedication of a mantelpiece in the White House in memory of her father. Her reply was short and to the point: "No, thank you." Later, Mrs. Kennedy sent her a photograph of the event with the President smiling broadly. She captioned it, "The Prez is delighted that he managed to get Mrs. L. to say a few words."

She also hated the idea of sounding like a pompous old dowager fingering her pearls and speaking in what she called "the fluffed-up tones" of a forgotten era. "Chirping away in a tumbril," she cheerfully commented on one tape I played back to her.

Several of the stories and descriptions she told on the tapes had already been published in her autobiography. Yet when you compare the written to the spoken version, the latter invariably holds up better. She told me once that she had hated writing *Crowded Hours* but had been forced to do so to help pay estate taxes when her husband died. "I wrote for profit, not literature," she said. Her writing was competent but lacked the sparkle and richness of her conversation. She really didn't enjoy writing her book, or the newspaper column she did in the early thirties, or even letters, of which she wrote very few.

She received a mountain of mail, nevertheless, and relished much of this one-sided correspondence, particularly the crank messages. She read me once with obvious delight a letter that began, "Dear Mrs. Shortworth, why has no one ever mentioned that your father had an illegitimate daughter by an Indian in North Dakota?"

She was by no means wedded to the past. One critic wrote that she had "moved into the White House when she was seventeen and never really let go of the place." This was a little unfair. She obviously liked being the daughter of a very popular President, the wife of a

Speaker of the House, and the perennial belle of the Washington social scene. But she seldom indulged in nostalgia. I doubt whether she enjoyed the White House years any more than any of the others. In fact, as she herself said, one of the reasons she married was to get away from it. What she did enjoy was the unique vantage point she had created for herself. She sat in the front row of the circus far longer than anyone else and was amused by the spectacle. She saw eighteen administrations come and go, and was privy to many secrets. She knew an enormously wide range of people, and was the privileged observer of many historical events. Yet all her life she remained healthily unimpressed by sacred cows in any shape or form.

It is difficult to know what political influence, if any, she exerted. She was the last person to be forthcoming in matters of this kind, although she did once tell me that she might be a "minor footnote" one day. Certainly she was influential with people like Henry Cabot Lodge, Sr., Senator Borah of Idaho, Senator Reed of Missouri, and John L. Lewis, President of the United Mineworkers of America. She shared a good many of their secrets and they respected her wide-ranging knowledge and astuteness, particularly about personalities. She had, by her own admission, "a simian ability to catch on." This, coupled with her firsthand knowledge of the Washington political scene, made her a shrewd and valued confidante to many of the leading figures of her day.

She was accused, especially by her family, of being publicity conscious—a terrible accusation to make in those days. Certainly she was always good copy, particularly as a young woman in the White House and again when she became "Washington's other monument" in her old age. She disdained the "Princess Alice" image. The idea of being considered a madcap "royal" when young and a "grande dame" when old never appealed to her. As with many who are put—or have put themselves—in the limelight, the distinction between the public image and the private view often becomes blurred.

She was also criticized for not having done anything particularly significant in her life, as, for instance, her cousin Eleanor Roosevelt had. She could hardly have been called a professional woman. In fact, when she died there was some doubt as to what exactly to write in the "profession or occupation" box on her death certificate. The authorities were adamant that it had to be completed and made various suggestions, including "housewife," which couldn't have been more ludicrously inappropriate. Finally Joanna's friend Robert Hellman came up with the suggestion of "gadfly" and this was accepted and duly recorded.

Certainly in the sense of echoing Socrates' belief that gadflies are necessary to sting the mule of society it couldn't have been more appropriate.

In many ways she was an intensely private and shy person. A lifetime of "showing off" had succeeded in masking her vulnerabilities to a great extent but not in disguising the real warmth and genuine feelings which lay underneath. Her formula of "shrugging a shoulder, raising an eyebrow, and showing a canine when necessary" had been honed to a fine art. But I wonder whether she ever fully appreciated how much pleasure she gave people.

A handicapped child once wrote to her asking for her philosophy of life and for a quotation which expressed it. In one of her rare letters she replied, "I don't think I have any philosophy of life but here is a quotation: 'A merry heart doeth good like a medicine: but a broken spirit drieth the bones'" (Proverbs 17:22).

M.T.

Childhood

The site of the house where I was born in New York was just about where Bergdorf Goodman is today. I must say I like the idea of being born under the counter at Bergdorf Goodman! It had been built by my Roosevelt grandfather.[8] His brother had a similar one next door. Fifty-seventh Street was way uptown then and they were real pioneers for those days, being so close to the park.

I have seen pictures of the interior of the house, which looks much more opulent and overwrought than the one my grandparents had on Twentieth Street, where my father was born. The two old Roosevelt peasants had obviously achieved burgherhood in their twin houses. They must have been frightfully pleased with themselves.

The month I was born in (February 1884) seems by all accounts to have been a strange one. The snows melted early, then more came. There was dense fog and a leaden, rather sinister atmosphere.

My parents had come to live on the third floor of the Fifty-seventh Street house shortly after they were married in October 1880. My father was spending a good deal of his time in Albany, where he was an assemblyman. He came to see my mother a few days before I was born, then returned to Albany. I was born on the evening of February 12. My mother began failing soon after. Apparently she had Bright's disease, which nobody had diagnosed. It could probably have been easily treated today.

My grandmother[9] was ill with typhoid on another floor of the house. My father knew this from my mother, who had written him that the doctors were worried about her but had given assurances that it was in no way catching. The whole thing seems to have been a medical fiasco. I have visions of everyone in long white nightgowns rushing hysterically between floors.

Alice Lee and Theodore Roosevelt. Boston. 1879

When my father finally arrived, he found both his wife and his mother dying in the same house. His father had died there almost on the same day six years previously. It is not surprising that my father insisted that there must be a curse on the place. It was all very macabre.

What little I know about the whole matter I learnt from my Aunt Gracie,[10] who was there throughout and left me a written description. It wasn't very illuminating but perhaps there was little to illumine. My mother apparently said something about how pleased she was that I was a girl, then sank back into a coma. The doctors huddled in corners. There was doubtless a lot of wringing of hands and deathbed watching. My grandmother and my mother died within hours of each other.

My father never told me anything about this. In fact, he never ever mentioned my mother to me, which was absolutely wrong. He never even said her name, or that I even *had* a different mother. He was so self-conscious about it. And my maternal grandparents,[11] with whom I stayed every year in Boston, never mentioned her either. Nor my aunts. Finally, Auntie Bye[12] did tell me something very revealing, such as that she had been very pretty and attractive. And she gave me some

The dining room of the Fifty-seventh Street house in New York

of her things . . . from my father I suppose . . . some of which (like the jewelry) were fun to have later on.

The whole thing was really handled very badly. It was awfully bad psychologically. There was I, laden with photographs of my late lamented mama, which I had to stick on my dressing table and on the wall above the bed. And I was always being exhorted, particularly by my Irish nurse, to "say a prayer for your little mother in heaven." It was all quite awful.

The impression I finally gleaned from others about her was that she was charming and frivolous and rather hideously Dickensian. Little Dora the child bride in fact. She came from a nice, proper, stuffy Bostonian background.

I have a whole batch of pictures of her with her Bostonian contemporaries and I must say in most of them she stands out as the prettiest. Shortly after her death my father gave Aunt Gracie what he said was his favorite photograph of her, which shows her aged about fourteen.

Apparently she was quite tall and slender, with blue-gray eyes and long blond hair, which tended to get over-wedged in structured waves. The Victorians seem to have had a thing about hair. They kept clipping it off as souvenirs of one thing or another. An aunt once referred to the beauty of my mother's "tendrils." I ask you! I was given some of my mother's and I was never sure what I was meant to do with them. There were far too many to stuff into a locket. Perhaps I should have worn them just once and given them all a "turn."

I don't think I would have liked my mother very much. Maybe it has something to do with the attitude the Roosevelts—along with most Victorians—had about the Little Woman and Large Families and the frail, lovely wife, who had to be protected and looked after. And then there was that awful sentimentality about the concept that you loved only once and you never loved again. It was pathetic, yet very tough at the same time. I think my father tried to forget he had ever been married to my mother. To blot the whole episode out of his mind. He didn't just never mention her to me, he never mentioned her name to *anyone*. Never referred to her ever again. It was most curious.

He obviously felt tremendously guilty about remarrying. A great friend of mine called Isabella Ferguson[13] told me that her mother remembered my father pacing up and down the room when he was staying with them after my mother died and saying, "I have no constancy. I wish I could be constant." He was obviously horrified by himself. The

Theodore Roosevelt's favorite picture of Alice Lee, aged fourteen

awful fidelity to the memory of the one who died! It is rather extraordinary that he should have felt that way because in those days they would have one wife, wear her out with childbearing and then take another when she died.

My father met my mother when he was at Harvard. The Lees lived next door to the Saltonstalls on Chestnut Hill and Richard Saltonstall, who was a classmate of my father's, was my mother's first cousin. He had a horse and trap and my father had a horse called Lightfoot, so between them they could easily cover the six miles between Harvard and Chestnut Hill. Froggy would a-wooing go!

One can follow the progress of my father's courtship of my mother from his diaries. All the ones relating to the years he knew my mother were given me when I was young, together with their correspondence. They make very sentimental reading. She was known as "Sunshine" in her family. He was very much the ardent suitor and his attachment to her became obsessive. Lightfoot must have become quite lame with all the hard riding he had to do! They seem always to have been on the point of swooning or giving indifferent poetry to each other.

Alice Lee in Boston before her marriage

Alice Lee (center right) with some of her Boston contemporaries, including Rose Saltonstall acting an improbable Delilah (top left)

Another group. Alice Lee center left and Rose Saltonstall right

I still have a book called *The Household Book of Verse*, which she gave him on their wedding day. It is a collection of dreary little Victorian poems full of sentiment and little else. It was all very "Little Womanish."

Finally they got married on October 27, 1880. It was his twenty-second birthday. She was nineteen. No wedding pictures have survived, if indeed any were taken. In fact, there are very few pictures of the two of them together at all. Early on in their relationship he begged her to come on a "tintype spree" with him and they did have a few taken together (although not tintypes), with the ever faithful Rose Saltonstall in attendance. She seems to have been my mother's constant companion, duenna, not to mention first cousin. There were also some pictures which were taken when a whole group of them went on a summer vacation to Mount Desert in Maine in the summer of 1879.

After my mother died, my father went out to his ranch in North Dakota and deposited me with my cherished Auntie Bye in New York. At least she quickly became cherished. She was the only one I really cared about when I was a child. She was certainly not beautiful . . . she was a great big handsome man of a woman . . . but oh so attractive! She was quite small in stature, yet she loomed large. She was both crippled (they said she had been dropped as a child, but I think it more likely that she had had infantile paralysis) and deaf, but somehow she managed to overcome these handicaps and certainly never made one aware of them.

Alice Lee and Rose Saltonstall by the sea in Maine. 1879

Alice Lee and Theodore Roosevelt and a group of his Harvard class-mates on Mount Desert Island, Maine. Summer of 1879

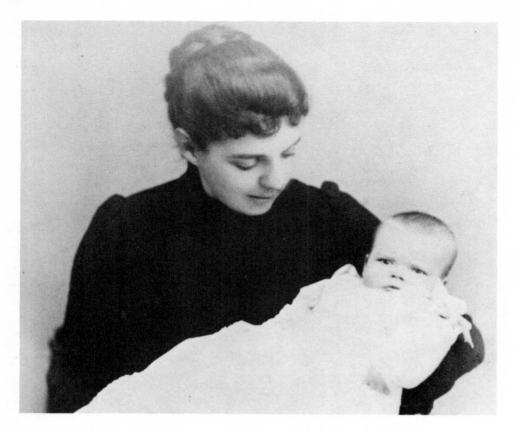

Tiny Alice with Auntie Bye. 1884

    She was the single most important influence on my childhood. I remember when my stepmother[14] came to New York after marrying my father. I was a child of three at the time and I was all dressed up in a most lovely dress . . . I still have the flounces of Valenciennes lace that trimmed it . . . and my curls were licked and prodded into place, and there was I at the top of the stairs at Auntie Bye's when the front door was opened and I had to descend into the hall with a large bunch of pink roses to greet my new mama. I remember my pleasure at having this enchanting dress and being told by the nurse how pretty I looked.

    Soon after that I must have been taken back by my father. My stepmother told me later that he wanted to leave me with Auntie Bye. Apparently he didn't want the symbol of his infidelity around, which explains why Auntie Bye was always telling me as a child, "Remember, darling, if you are very unhappy you can always come back to me." She was really rather possessive about me and could be quite tough with my father on the subject. She called me her "blue-eyed darling," can you believe, and she protected me from my father with his guilt fetish, and from my stepmother, and even from myself. She was an extraordinary woman.

Who knows, if my father had succeeded in giving me away to his sister, I would probably be the nonagenarian great-grandmother of Vanderbilts and Astors today, and would be living in some costly New York hotel, instead of a nice old shabby home in Washington.

Auntie Bye spoilt me. And so did my maternal grandparents in Boston. For a long time I was their only grandchild. Their youngest child was barely fifteen when I began spending my vacations with them, so they had a lot to put up with, especially as I tended to be defiant from the beginning. In the first place I considered them to be frightfully stuffy. My grandfather was very proud of his Cabot connections and the Lees considered themselves rather special, despite the fact that they were not the right Lees, because the right Lees were all wrong because they were Southerners.

I went to my grandparents for three weeks in the spring and another three in the fall. I used to be sent to them with a nurse, who then returned to Sagamore, so I left for three enchanting weeks with everyone trying to make me deliriously happy. I was treated there as *belonging*. Everything belonged to me. I would come in and jump up and down on the sofa, hoping the springs would break, and they would merely smile indulgently.

We used to have wonderfully made toys as children but not very many of them. We had giant bricks to build houses with. They used to come in large boxes which came by wagon. There were also windows and doors that came with them, but no glass. I also remember a firehouse that had scaled fire engines inside.

In one of the middle rooms of the Beacon Street house there was a wonderful doll's house that had belonged to my mother, and I used to play with that for hours. I also had my mother's dolls with dresses done in the period when she was a child. They were known as Alice's dolls and they gave me a great deal of pleasure for many years. I still have my own childhood doll's house, which was given me when I was about six by my Grandfather Lee, and I have added considerably to its furniture over the years. I enjoy rearranging it to this day.

In the winter my grandparents lived on Beacon Street. It wasn't as grand as Beacon Hill itself but it did show that Lee Higginson & Co., my grandfather's firm, made money. One of the few recollections I have of the house is how cold it could be, especially the bedrooms and the rooms in the rear overlooking Back Bay. They fairly radiated Puritan Ethic in their frigidity. Poor old Uncle George and Aunt Hattie (the two youngest children of my grandparents) used to creep down to breakfast blue with cold every morning. The rooms in the front got the sun and were much larger and brighter.

I also always associate Thanksgiving in the Beacon Street house with masses of food, which Grandma Lee particularly relished. She was a great eater. I used to save the wishbones from the turkeys because my aunts used to make me wonderful witchlike figures out of them, using sealing wax for their heads. They also used to make me the most beautiful scrapbooks.

Lee Higginson & Co. were bankers and I suppose my grandfather was vaguely prosperous. Certainly he gave me a generous allowance when I was young. I still have some of his letters where, in a small, meticulous hand, he would outline some financial arrangement he was organizing for my benefit. Invariably he would add the cautionary note, "Don't tell your grandmother about this."

When I was a little older, I learnt from heaven knows where about the difference between leaving money *per stirpes* as opposed to *per capita*. And I constantly reminded my grandfather of it. "Remember, Grandpa," I would say, "*per stirpes*, not *per capita*." I must really have been an odious child but I don't think he minded. Anyway it worked, because when he came to set up trust funds just before he died, he divided the money between his five children in equal lots and I got all of my mother's share. I don't suppose many children would have thought of things like that. It must have been my good, frugal, yet *greedy* New England ancestors coming out in me.

I remember my grandfather better than my grandmother. He was small, rather dapper, and pleasantly cheerful. He had closely cropped white hair, very bright blue eyes, and he loved to tease. I think that is why my grandmother had a perpetually harassed expression. I can see him now returning in the evening to the house on Chestnut Hill, wearing a small straw boater and carrying the evening paper under his arm. I often used to go down to the station to meet him.

Grandma Lee was a fellow New Englander. She came from New Bedford. I believe her family home is still there. She had worried brown eyes, a puzzled expression, and she frequently suffered from

With Grandmother Lee and her young cousin, Caroline Fessenden

"turns" of one sort or another, so she spent a lot of time in her room. I can't ever remember seeing her wear anything but black. She even came to my wedding wearing black, which struck me as a little strange, especially as she was most definitely not a widow at the time. She outlived my grandfather by quite a few years. Perhaps the influence of Queen Victoria was more ubiquitous than anyone thought.

The Chestnut Hill house was pleasant and unpretentious and had a large lawn which faded away to a tennis court. Or was it a vegetable garden? I can still conjure up the smell of the house, which was a mixture of fresh linen and waxed floors and camphor.

The Saltonstalls lived right next door and there was a side gate between the two properties, so there was a lot of coming and going and guests at one house were automatically shared with the other. That is how my father met my mother.

Nearby there were other neighbors such as Alice and George West and Mr. and Mrs. John Lowell, whose daughter became a good friend of mine. Further up the road a number of other Lee relations also had houses. It was all very tribal.

Boardwalks had to be laid down between the various houses to provide ease of access, especially in rainy weather when the roads became very muddy.

I loved it there because I had much more freedom and could do exactly as I pleased. I ran wild there and really hated to go back to Sagamore and the dreary round of tea in the playroom with crustless brown bread instead of the delicious French rolls I had become accustomed to at the Lees'. It was that kind of difference.

My grandmother used to take me back on the railroad and the moment I got home I would start crying and sniffling. For at least three days I was desperately homesick for my grandparents. My stepmother —not to mention the nurse—always complained how unsettling these trips to Boston made me.

I was conscious from an early age that I had one set of different relatives from my brothers and sisters. I had Grandpa and Grandma Lee and a posse of Lee aunts and uncles. They had their Carow relations, including a grandmother called Gertrude[15] who was a venerable-looking old lady, invariably dressed in white. I always confused her with the Pope. I believe she was in fact a converted Catholic.

They didn't feed the children on formulas in those days and my brother Ted found out . . . from one of the nurses, doubtless . . . that after my mother died I had had a wet nurse for a time. So this horrid

Grandfather Lee opens Boston's first underground safe-deposit vaults

The Lee house at Chestnut Hill near Boston. Alice in foreground

little cross-eyed boy of about five would go around to all and sundry exclaiming, "Sissy had a sweat nurse! Sissy had a sweat nurse!" It was frightfully wounding to the character! It's not surprising that early on I became fairly hard-minded and learnt to shrug a shoulder with indifference. I certainly wasn't going to be part of everyone saying, "the poor little thing."

I think my mother had been well educated but without much taste. Unlike my stepmother, who had great literary taste and *cared* for things. I think she thought my father's family were all uneducated Dutch peasants.

I was called Alice after my mother but never really liked the name. If she had lived I have the horrible vision of there being a Big Alice and a Little Alice. She in turn had been named after her maternal grandmother, Alice Hathaway.

I got saddled with the Lee name as well—those nice New England Tory Lees, most of whom seem to have gone to Canada during the Revolution. They were very properly Boston, perfectly well educated, but without any claims to culture. They went to Harvard, joined the right clubs. All that. I was really very fond of them. At least they were *mine* and I didn't have to share them with my siblings.

The Lees included a lot of Roses. Harriet Rose was my great-grandmother. The Roses brought a very blond, very blue-eyed look into the family—and into the Saltonstalls as well, come to think of it. Originally, they had come to New England via Antigua in the West Indies. I remember when my cousin Reginald Gray went down there to trace some of his Caribbean relatives, he found that the blond Nordic look had yielded to very much duskier complexions, which filled me with glee but which caused a certain amount of, shall we say, pursed-lipped concern among my respectable New England relations. The Roosevelts seem to have been every bit as respectable as the Lees. I once told a writer, who was doing something on the family, that "The origins of the Roosevelts are obscure," which is true enough.

They took their lineage seriously and sported coats of arms, etc., when they became burghers and men of property. The name meant "field of roses" in Dutch, so we had roses in book plates and crested rings (including one worn by my father, much to my disdain). Roosevelt babies always had cascades of roses tumbling down their christening robes. Franklin even incorporated the "Roosevelt" three ostrich feathers—without any reference to the Prince of Wales—into the White House china when he was President.

Some say the Roosevelts were entitled to coats of arms. Others thought they were one step ahead of the bailiffs from an island in the Zuider Zee. Certainly their heraldry would not, I think, have survived the scrutiny of the College of Arms.

I hate to think of my Roosevelt forebears as being nothing but sturdy Dutch burghers. There was German and French and English blood as well. Perhaps, as some fat Dutch ancestress of mine was fleeing from the Spanish army, she looked back and was caught up by a Moor, who brought a little Mediterranean levity into our lives.

My grandfather Roosevelt's marriage to my Southern grandmother introduced some new blood, and the subsequent conflicts between the Dutch, New England, and "Georgia cracker" sides of our personalities have been rewarding.

My grandfather seems to have been a person of considerable character. All his children were devoted to him. He died when they were quite young and my father took years to get over it.

Auntie Bye would tell me lovely stories of their father feeding them from a great box of peaches at Tranquillity, their country home on Long Island. They would have to lie on their tummies on the edge of a piazza so as not to let the juice drop on them. He was devoted to his family, although the strains of being married to a Southerner—and a fervid Southerner at that—must have been trying at times, especially during the Civil War.

There was my grandmother with two brothers fighting on the Confederate side (they were both on the *Alabama*). They were on the proscribed list, and even after the war had to come to New York under assumed names. Apparently things became so tense that family reunions at the Twentieth Street house in New York were canceled for the duration of the war. My grandmother seems to have spent most of this time having the "vapors" in her room with her sister, Anna Bulloch, and her mother for company. Anna was the typical decorous old maid aunt, although she later married and we had an Uncle Gracie as well as an Aunt Gracie after that.

As a personality, my grandmother doesn't stand out as much a character as my grandfather. From her pictures, and from what little I learnt from Auntie Bye, she was extremely beautiful with great charm of manner when she wanted to exercise it. She also seems to have been moody, temperamental and, like most hypochondriacs, she enjoyed poor health. One heard stories of her covered with veils and dust coat venturing forth in the summer heat and with cuffs of brown paper to prevent even the slightest speck of dust besmirching her. It all sounds rather obsessive.

I know very little about her except one of her Bulloch ancestors was the first president of the Provincial Congress of Georgia. The correspondence between her and her children is so overcharged with sentimentality that it is difficult to read. For me, at any rate. They called her pet names such as "Motherkins" and "Little Motherling" and then my father, after a year's schooling in Germany, produced "Maueschen" and other blush-making horrors, which aroused every bit of the New England peasant in me and made me want to dry my hands.

Despite this show of sentiment and affection, I get the impression that my father was not nearly so devoted to his mother as he was to his father. Of the two, she seems to have been the more distant.

Whatever the reason, Auntie Bye, from a very early age, became

Tranquillity, the Roosevelt summer house at Oyster Bay, with Edith Carow (right) and Corinne Roosevelt sitting on the lawn

Bulloch Hall in Roswell, Georgia, childhood home of Theodore Roose-velt's mother, Martha Bulloch

an important factor in the organization of the family and, after their father's death, it was she who became, to a great extent, the controlling one. She always had great responsibilities in her family. Or had assumed them because of her rather vague, delicate, and fanciful Southern mother.

There is a charming story of Auntie Bye as a child with her nurse Dora, who was also my father's nurse. They were going somewhere and Auntie Bye, a very *bustling* little girl, wanted to pack her own trunk, so she said, "Doh pack Doh trunk, Bye pack Bye trunk."

There is always someone in every family who keeps it together. In ours, it was Auntie Bye. I always believed that if she had been a man she, rather than my father, would have been President.

I went to her almost immediately after my mother died and stayed until 1887, after my father remarried. One of my earliest memories is of seeing her bustle hanging in her bedroom in New York. Up to that point, I always considered it an integral part of her anatomy. I was absolutely horrified when I saw it as a separate entity and thought it had been chopped off her by force.

Another memory is of being carried by her butler Chamberlain to see the sunset at Sagamore. He was very tall (tall butlers were eagerly sought after in those days and were paid more than the average-size ones). And he had enormous side whiskers, which fascinated me.

Chamberlain also took me once to the window of Auntie Bye's Madison Avenue house during the great blizzard of March 1888 and he told me to memorize the scene because I would never see the likes of it again. Since it was difficult to see out because of the swirling wall of snow, it wasn't an easy instruction to follow.

Auntie Bye had an extraordinary gift with people. She had an enormous range of friends of all shapes and sizes. She enjoyed all types. Father had the same quality but because my stepmother was "anti-fashionable," so to speak, he was more restricted in whom he saw. Auntie Bye was not. She didn't feel that being fashionable was necessarily a little shady.

Her house on the corner of Sixty-second Street and Madison Avenue in New York was really home for me as a child. I can remember the lovely smell of baking bread coming from the kitchen. Auntie Bye's food was invariably good—by far the best in our family. It was she who introduced me to the pleasure of English-style afternoon tea with piping-hot Earl Grey's tea and lots of paper-thin bread and butter. She

Auntie Bye with three-year-old Alice. 1887

Alice with baby Ted. 1888

spent a long time in England and picked up a number of English habits. For instance, she had accumulated a slightly different style of handwriting, which I valiantly tried to imitate with singular lack of success.

One of my favorite pictures of her is when she was dressed up prior to being presented to Queen Victoria. She looks unfazed by the imposing conformity of her court dress. It also shows what a nice handsome North American face she had in an age when all her contemporaries were desperately striving to look like Lillie Langtry or the Princess of Wales.

My father's great friend Cecil Spring-Rice,[16] whom we knew as "Springy," did a charming caricature of Auntie Bye's presentation at court. So did my brother Ted. We thought the whole thing very comic but were impressed nonetheless.

Springy was one of the pleasures of my childhood. He had been the best man at my father's wedding in 1886. I can remember him as a child bringing bunches of wild flowers and helping me plait them into the cane bottoms of the nursery chairs to add an air of fantasy to our otherwise mundane surroundings. He was also a great source of rhymes and limericks and other marvels.

Auntie Bye all dressed up to be presented to Queen Victoria

Alice Roosevelt with her two brothers, Kermit and Ted (right)

I think the only two holidays we spent as a family together were organized by Auntie Bye, who took us for two weeks to Lake Champlain and for another two weeks to Bennington, Vermont.

Both Auntie Bye and Auntie Corinne[17] were great at giving parties. Theirs were the only ones I remember as a child. I never had any *young* good times at parties except with them.

Auntie Corinne had the same sort of vitality and enthusiasm as Auntie Bye, although in her case it could be more contrived. For instance, she had a great facility for feigning interest. It was known as her "elbow-in-the-soup treatment." We were left speechless with admiration at her ability to show interest in some bore's discourse. With her elbow almost stuck into her soup plate, she would gaze at him—or her—intently hanging onto every word. It was a magnificent performance.

She came unstuck with Queen Mary, though. It was at a reception at Buckingham Palace, shortly after George V had ascended the throne. He and Queen Mary had just returned from the Delhi Durbar in India and the Queen was describing how one night, in her vast, ornate tent, she had heard "a most curious noise." Auntie Corinne, eager to learn the denouement of the story, leant forward and said, "What

Eleanor Roosevelt with her two brothers, Elliott and Hall (right)

was it, Ma'am, what was it?" Queen Mary, obviously annoyed at having her story anticipated in this way, drew herself up to her full height and said very coldly, "It could have been a wolf. Good evening." And then sailed on majestically, leaving a crushed Auntie Corinne in her wake.

Auntie Bye entertained quite a lot at Sagamore before my father remarried. She moved there just as it was being finished and there was a wonderful feeling of warmth and ease and hospitality when she was there, which was never quite the case with my stepmother. She always had a lot of her friends around and a number of attractive young men who were known to us as Joe-Bobs after two of her best friends, Bob Ferguson, who was a Scot and a Rough Rider, and Joe Alsop, who married my cousin Corinne Robinson. But that all came a bit later than the 1880 period. Auntie Bye was married at the end of 1895 to Admiral William Cowles, known to us as Uncle Will. We were absolutely flabbergasted when she took this adventuresome step at the advanced age of forty-one and even more so when, three years later, the Life Force having demanded that she produce a child, out popped young Sheffield Cowles in time to see the admiral off to Cuba in 1898.

There is a revealing picture of Auntie Bye with me, which was taken when I was about three. It shows her hovering over me in a loving way while I am staring directly ahead looking vaguely defiant.

There is another taken a little later with me standing with one hand on my belly. I was chided about that. "Disrespectful," they said, "to put your hand on your stomach like that." Disrespectful, I ask you!

I look rather baleful if not downright insolent in most of these early pictures. "A disapproving eye and a damned disinheriting countenance," as Sheridan said. I remember being tremendously concerned about my hair. Auntie Bye used to let me put it forward and curled it to cover my high forehead, which I was ashamed of. Others, like Grandma Lee, caught me later and made me draw it back, revealing my True Nature. I remember the nurse curling my hair around a long stick. Nobody gave me bangs, worse luck, except when I was very small.

I also had a battle over footwear. Whereas other children had nice slippers—at least part of the time anyway—I was forced, for "orthopedic reasons," they said, to wear ugly black boots *and* braces, which I used to take off and hit the other children with. The braces were certainly due to the aftereffects of polio, which they didn't know how to diag-

The "disrespectful" picture, aged four

nose or to treat in those days. At the age of about two, I was carried screaming to the carriage by the nurse and taken to hospital. The doctor advised the stretching of one leg, which was shorter than the other by about one inch, and the correction of my feet, which stuck out at different angles. It didn't hurt very much but then I seemed to have been somewhat physically insensitive from birth. Every evening the Achilles tendons were stretched by my stepmother, who spent five minutes on one leg and seven and a half minutes on the other. She felt it was her duty to do this for me, she didn't trust the nurse to do it. At least the whole gruesome procedure taught me to stand up straight as I was practically a cripple.

My stepmother made an enormous effort with me as a child but I think she was bored by doing so. We became very good friends. She was New England with a French Huguenot background and I was half New England. We laughed at the same things. But she could be mean.

She let it be known that my father had proposed to her before he met my mother. Certainly they had known each other since childhood. There is a charming and rather interesting picture of Lincoln's funeral procession passing my great-grandfather's house in New York and if one looks very closely one can see two small heads watching from a second-floor window. Presumably they are my father and his younger brother, Elliott. My stepmother was also there but apparently she cried so much at the sight of the procession, they shut her up in the back room to keep her quiet.

My father and she had been close and certainly there was some romantic interest there. It was taken for granted by his family that they would marry. And then he went to Harvard and met my mother, fell in love with her, and married. After my mother died he fell in love again—really in love—with my stepmother. For a time they didn't want to see each other. There was definitely something there. I suppose they must have seen each other during the time he was married to my mother because she was a great friend of his sisters, particularly Aunt Corinne. I have a photograph taken in Canada in the early 1880's which shows my stepmother, Bye, Corinne, and my mother together with a number of others on a skating trip to Montreal. I think it must be the only picture of my mother and my stepmother taken together.

My stepmother's family was good, impoverished New England stock. Her father had what is usually referred to as "a drinking problem," i.e , he was an alcoholic. He died when she and her sister were still quite

Edith Roosevelt in 1900

30

Lincoln's funeral procession passes the Roosevelt house in New York, April 1865. A young Theodore Roosevelt and his brother Elliott watch from the second-floor window (circle)

Alice Lee Roosevelt (third from left, center row) and Edith Carow (top row right) with companions on a skating trip to Canada. 1883

Edith Roosevelt's mother, Gertrude Carow

Sagamore Hill. Alice's bedroom

The North Room

The house in summer

And in winter

young and the family went to live in Europe. They were the kind of Americans who lived abroad because they could live quite nicely on a *tiny* income in Paris, Rome, or Florence.

Her early years had been unhappy, which could account for her withdrawn, rather parched quality. I remember Aunt Corinne, who was one of her closest friends, telling me that they were rather concerned when she married my father, because they feared she would come between him and the family. She did in a way. She had a tendency to say things like, "Theodore, I think we've seen quite enough of Corinne and Douglas and I don't think we'll ask them down for a while." And that was that. My father on occasion did put his foot down but it was she who usually called the shots in these matters. She was a beautiful woman with a most unusual face. She had slightly Semitic features, derived perhaps from a Phoenician strain through her Welsh relations. Or perhaps Aaron Burr's side of the family had something to do with it. He was a distant relation.

However, Roosevelt peasant stock won out as the dominant strain in her children, with the exception of Archie, who was born looking like Bernie Baruch.

She was a pleasure and I was devoted to her. You couldn't match her for all kinds of things and we shared many of the same interests, especially literary. It was said that in some respects I was more like her than her own children. But then the same sort of thing was said about my cousin Eleanor being more like my father's daughter than I was. Odious comparisons that added nothing to family solidarity!

She was a great admirer of Henry Adams and was very much a part of his circle. I don't think I could have stood those literary gatherings with "Uncle Henry," as he was called, surrounded by a host of adoring "nieces" mouthing Dante and medieval Latin hymns and things like that. There was also a lot of genuflecting around the rather curious statue that he had erected in Rock Creek cemetery in memory of his wife, who, it is said, committed suicide because he was in love with another woman. Ugh!

My stepmother was terribly conscientious about me. She had insisted on keeping me with them when they married. My father obviously didn't want the symbol of his infidelity around. His *two* infidelities, in fact: infidelity to my stepmother by marrying my mother first, and to my mother by going back to my stepmother after she died. It was all so dreadfully Victorian and mixed up. My stepmother added a typically caustic twist by telling my brother Ted, who naturally

Edith Roosevelt with Archie. 1897

repeated it to me, that it was just as well that my mother had died when she did because my father would have been bored to death staying married to her. I think she always resented being the second choice and she never really forgave him his first marriage. In many ways she was a very hard woman. She was Jonathan Edwards stock and she had almost a gift for making her own people uncomfortable.

Although my earliest memories were mostly of Auntie Bye's house in New York, Sagamore featured early too. The house was finished shortly after my mother's death. Originally, it was to have been called Leeholm but they quickly changed that when my mother died. Auntie Bye really took over the running of the house when my father went out to the North Dakota ranch after my mother's death.

Sagamore is an ugly house of that period. My father was near-sighted and I think the place looked small to him, so he indulged himself by building on the big north room after he became President. Originally the house had yellow shingles with red trim but my stepmother

Ted

Ethel and Kermit

had it painted all gray. The setting is quite lovely with beautiful views, especially in the fall, across to Connecticut. There were always pleasant breezes running through the house.

My father used to love standing on the piazza, which is something quite different from a porch, in the evening to watch the sunset and the boats go tooting by.

The house was late Victorian, which was not the most attractive period. It remains very much as it was. Nothing substantial was changed there in my stepmother's time, and she only died in 1948. For instance, there was no electricity there until 1914. The north room was full of tusks and odd round chairs, which for some reason or other had something to do with Dutch sea captains.

The thing that attracted me most was the bedroom set in the main bedroom, which was perfectly fascinating. It had been given to my grandfather and was of curly maple, Gothic enough to hang bells on, with squares and octagons of dark wood inlaid in light wood. We used to hang our stockings from the bed at Christmas.

The great white sarcophagus of a bath in the only bathroom in the house was the other thing I loved. It was a wonderful place to luxuriate in, with its piles of towels marked "R of S" (Roosevelt of Sagamore), to distinguish them from the laundry of the Yellowbanks Roosevelts, who lived nearby and were good, solid, *rich* cousins of one degree or another.

They rise before my scornful but envious eyes. They kept on marrying frightfully respectable and grand people . . . a succession of little senators from New Jersey and their old maid sisters. They were so rich that they could scarcely manage to spend the income of the income of the year before. That kind of thing.

The gunroom at the top of the house was Father's particular preserve. It was the one room in the house which we didn't venture into uninvited. We used to play hide-and-go-seek there and all my father had to do was to growl and moan and we would rush away in terror. It was a horrid, savage noise that quite petrified us.

The guns there were not just decorative. We had rifles pressed into our tiny paws at a tender age. I can see us on the piazza shooting at railings or a fence, much to my stepmother's horror. There was a lovely place that looked like a valley with a road running through two meadowish hills. We would shoot at the number of targets across the valley to the peril of any poor soul venturing along the road.

Then there were all those outdoor sports and games. The Kennedys with their touch football had nothing to the goings-on at Saga-

The family at Sagamore. Alice on the right

A handicap race around the barn with T.R. doing the timing

more. One of my earliest memories of my father was his coming back from hunting with a broken arm and a bloody nose. I started screaming at this apparition and he started shaking me to shut me up, which only made me scream more. So he shook more. It was a theme which was to be repeated, with variations, in later years.

I was always frightened by riding but managed to master the elements. I was really a physical coward when I was a child. I wasn't flexible that way. I was very envious of Nancy Astor, for instance, because she could turn cartwheels and I couldn't. I could always do yoga and pop my leg behind my head and things like that but that's just relaxing. And although I like swimming, I couldn't dive. I can see my father at Sagamore shouting to me from the water, "Dive, Alicy, dive." And there was I trembling on the bank saying through tears, "Yes, Father," to this sea monster who was flailing away in the water, peering near-sightedly at me without glasses and with his mustache glistening wet in the sunlight. It was pathetic. My cousin Eleanor was always so fine about that sort of thing. She hated it as much as I did but was much more unprotesting. I was not. I cried. I snarled. I hated.

Oh, those perfectly awful endurance tests masquerading as games! They were rugged to a degree. Very good, I suppose, if one didn't cut oneself to pieces. I cut my head open once somersaulting down Cooper's Bluff at Sagamore . . . a favorite site for our handicap races . . . and had to be driven to the village by my parents in order to have my head sewn up.

Some of our games, however, were great fun. There was a large oak tree at Sagamore and my father used to haul us up to the lowest branches by a rope tied to our feet or in my case around my middle because my braces, which stretched from ankle to knee, were a hindrance. And there were lovely long "scrambly" walks and rowing picnics to Lloyd's Neck and other spots in Cold Spring Harbor where we baked clams on the beach and ate jelly sandwiches and hard-boiled eggs.

We had very simple food at Sagamore. My father always liked, by his own admission, "coarse food and plenty of it." So it was lots of mashed potatoes and string beans and roast beef on Sundays and fresh oysters on occasion. There was a lovely dish with eggplant but Father considered that rather fussy. We had a flourishing vegetable garden and we always had loads of things like corn and spinach—great big green spinach not delicately prepared and disguised.

Food was rather different in those days because it was so seasonal—

for instance, we grabbed at asparagus when it was in season. Perhaps it is my imagination but it seems to me that food used to have more taste and flavor. In its natural state, that is.

I don't think my stepmother had a tremendous interest in food except to feed us healthily, and she really did a great job in running a household on a comparatively small budget.

I don't have much recollection of salads or cheeses but we did have delicious homemade ice cream and masses of fresh fruit. We had a wonderful orchard with cherries and pears and apples of all kinds. We also had a grape arbor and strawberry beds. I used to spend a lot of time daydreaming in the apple orchard or down in the mossy glades of the woods. I assumed the ownership of the orchard and every year my siblings had to pay their dues by climbing a tree for me.

Before the advent of the refrigerator we were really quite restricted in what we could keep. Large hunks of ice were cut from the pond and then put in the icehouse and kept covered with sawdust throughout the summer.

I also associate pitchers of lemonade with summer. It seemed to be always on tap and we had it after games, like tennis, with plenty of sugar in it. I adored it.

We were quite close as a family but inevitably there was pairing off. Ted and I, for instance, were boon companions and shared many of the same interests. Kermit couldn't have been more fun, especially as he grew older. He paired off with Ethel. Quentin and Archie were "the little boys." Quentin in particular had tremendous charm and I was devoted to him . . . and that's not just because he was killed in the war.[18]

Archie and I had a few brushes when we were young. I recall once when I had gone down into the pantry at Sagamore to fetch something and Archie came in and said, "Look at Sissy in the cupboard, *eating*." So naturally when I climbed down my foot happened to hit his mouth and there were screams of rage.

My brothers could be mean to both Ethel and me but very rarely to themselves. I suppose that is true in many families.

Kermit and I shared a common passion for gypsies. We had been brought up on Borrow[19] and we knew quite a number of them in Washington. Pennsylvania Avenue had several houses which were owned and occupied by gypsies in the winter, their "bad weather time." We used to visit them there and also at the encampment they used to have near the Benning racetrack, and we learned a certain amount of Romany to converse with them in.

Quentin in the garden

Kermit could be very amusing to be with. I once nearly drowned with him at a swamp near Auntie Bye's house in Farmington in Connecticut and all he kept saying rather plaintively after the mishap was "What will Father say when he hears two of his children have drowned?"

I don't suppose any parent ever participated more actively in the pastimes of his children than my father did. He seemed to be involved in everything. And when he wasn't around, he wrote us the most wonderful picture letters. They were full of life. The men strolled and the horses galloped and they were just delightful. After he became President we used to say, "Do us one of those so we can cash them in later." We called them "posterity letters."

He was an incredible father and great fun. He was never mean. Well, not really mean. Just noble mean on occasion.

We were a reading family and both my father and stepmother encouraged us at an early age to read. They were also very good at reading aloud to us, with my stepmother concentrating on Walter Scott's

And in a 1906 portrait

poems and Maria Edgeworth's tales, whereas my father belted out lots of British ballads and Longfellow's *The Saga of King Olaf*, and the *Nibelungenlied*, a nice savage saga, which we all shouted out with glee.

Kipling was a particular favorite. I remember him coming to lunch once . . . was it in Washington or Sagamore? . . . and my brother Ted, who was about seven at the time, insisted on reciting *The Ballad of East and West* just to show that he knew it. I could have managed a poem or two but was too shy to try it. Not Ted. And I can remember Kipling glowering and raising his tremendous eyebrows with what we hoped was surprise and delight at Ted's performance.

Father was a very quick reader. Both he and Auntie Bye were also very good at giving you a picture of what they had read in their own words. They were not hampered by verbal memory as are so many people, who can memorize easily but then are not able to put it into their own words afterwards.

I had very little formal education, which saved a lot of excitement for my later years. I'm really just inquisitive with a simian ability to catch on. My father read all the time, so I just followed his example. What is more, I read largely what I wanted with very little guidance. There were some lovely books on astronomy which fascinated me. I also enjoyed Greek grammar. Latin I was made to study and consequently didn't enjoy much. I did Caesar and then, having tried to throw a number of winter quarters across the Rhine, stopped. Kermit was the Greek scholar in our family and Ted the Latin one. We sat pouring *larmes* over *"La Grecque sans larmes."* And I was also taught French and some German.

I belong to the Andrew Lang period of *The Blue Fairy Book*, which was marvelous folklore with charming illustrations. It's surprising how few really good American children's books there were when I was growing up. We were supposed not to read Louisa May Alcott because the writing was so bad. Mrs. Molesworth was much more acceptable. And books like *The Tapestry Room* and *Children of the Castle* were enchanting. *Uncle Tom's Cabin* was just there. We didn't have any encouragement about it. *Black Beauty* was considered terribly sentimental and *Little Lord Fauntleroy* was not even allowed in the house because it was so dreadful. That awful child being frightfully condescending to everyone including Grandfather Dear, ugh! Now, Franklin was *encouraged* to read *Little Lord Fauntleroy* as a child. We even suspected

Alice reading. 1891

he dressed a little like him. It was *that* kind of difference which manifested itself at an early age.

We were lightly nudged towards Mark Twain, even though my father thought he was a vulgar old horror. I remember seeing him from time to time, usually in a crumpled, stained white linen suit. There was something slightly demeaning about enjoying Mark Twain. We had Dickens every moment. Also Scott's Waverley Novels.

Lord Dunsany was a particular friend. His books delighted my youth. There was one called *Gods of Pegana* and another entitled *The Book of Wonder*. He wrote very peculiar short, short stories which were pagan to a degree and wonderfully illustrated.

I remember one about the woman who went to an idol shop and asked for a god she could worship when it was wet. She was reminded of the penalties attached to idolatry but she still insisted, "Give me a god to worship when it is wet." So she was given a god named "The God of Raining Cheerfulness," which she happily took home to worship. There we are. We absolutely love gods to worship.

Dunsany was immensely tall. He was also a superb shot and at his home in Ireland, which was a faintly castle-ish thing, he used to lie back on the lawn and shoot at the doorbell until someone came out and gave him what he wanted. Oh, the eccentrics of yesteryear!

He turned up in Cincinnati once and when I drove him around the city at an average speed of about eighty miles an hour, as was my custom, he said, "You had better be careful or you will find you will go to meet up with the gods before you wish to."

I loved astronomy from an early age. It appealed to my imagination. Father was particularly good at conjuring up the dawn of time for us. So much of our modern world seems so very trivial in comparison. The almost childlike enjoyment I take in subjects like astronomy— geology is another—has carried through into my old age. Hubble said he had never spent a better night in a telescope (the hundred-inch at Mount Wilson in California) than with me because it excited me so.

Our governesses were very good. There were two of them. The nursery one for the little boys and one for the older ones. I can see Mademoiselle Drouet eating with the children while Miss Young was comfortably here with us.

We were always expected to be very polite to the servants. Father was particularly chivalrous and there was a Tolstoian moment at Sagamore when he proposed calling all the maids "Miss Annie" or whatever, but my stepmother scoffed at the idea.

The family in 1897

An Irish nurse called Mame was the one who loomed largest in my childhood. She had come to us when my stepmother married my father and she had been her nurse and also that of her brother, poor little Uncle Kermit, who had died in infancy. So she went way back into the nineteenth century. Her real name was Mary Ledwith and she was a delight. She had a curiously austere and ascetic face . . . not unlike a priest's . . . which belied her great warmth of character. She could be both strict and charming, an ideal combination in a nurse. We loved her. She suffered from something which was known rather lugubriously as "milk leg," because mothers got it from nursing their babies. And sweat nurses, too, presumably. It was probably a case of varicose veins. Anyway I can see Mame now in her lilac-colored elastic stockings for her "milk leg" driving off with us in the pony cart at Sagamore.

She succeeded an earlier nurse I had, called Ginny Jane, who was also Irish. It was from her that I picked up a splendid Irish brogue. I was sitting one day at Sagamore mourning over a toy goat I had, saying in my childish Irish brogue, "And he lost *ahl* its legs and *ahl* its fur and *ahl* its horns. And that's the way the goat went." My father loved to tell the tale of this gloomy child of five contemplating the demise of her toy goat.

Another very early memory was being knocked down by two shaggy wolfhounds which my father had brought back from the ranch in North Dakota. Dogs were an integral part of our household when I was a child along with a variety of other pets.

The Irish accent was superseded by an English intonation, which was partly New England creeping in and partly the influence of our English governess, who also taught me to mumble in the inimitable English way on occasion (usually when I'm bored). But I also learned to bellow. I was always being sent out to the piazza to call up transportation. "Sister," they would say, "go out and call for the carriage now." As the stables were fully a quarter of a mile away, it was quite a lungful. My brothers called me Sister or Sissy. Later on their children (and their descendants) called me Auntie Sister, which was a Southern, faintly coy thing.

A good deal of my early childhood was spent in the country. We lived in Washington for five years from 1889 but continued to spend a lot of time at Sagamore. In 1895 we moved to New York, when my father was made Police Commissioner. We lived at Auntie Bye's because she was in London then. I have only a few hazy memories of that period but I can remember my father in street clothes (instead of dinner things) prior to going out on one of his nocturnal rambles in the tenement house districts. A bit like Gladstone and the prostitutes, only my father wouldn't have appreciated the allusion.

From New York, we moved back to Washington, when Father became Assistant Secretary of the Navy. The first time I had been there was when I was about six and I was taken to see President Harrison, who appeared to me a gnarled, bearded gnome of a man gloomily ensconced in a corner of the Red Room at the White House.

Washington seemed extraordinarily quiet compared to New York. It was a village really. I remember driving up from the station in a thing called a herdic, which was like a small horse-drawn bus. I felt like a tenement child, still in my leg braces. The streets were quiet and tree-lined and the atmosphere that of a postbellum Southern town. It was a town clustered around a small center. There was the Octagon House, then I Street with the home of the two Misses Riggs of the bank, Justice Gray's house, K Street, which was fairly grown up. Then there was a street of nothing in particular. Then the Storer house, Massachusetts Avenue, Senator Lodge's (where the Brookings Institute is now), Winthrop House, where old Harry du Pont lived, and Stewart Castle on Dupont

Mame and Quentin

Circle, which was an old, rather battered frame house built by a Western senator.

When I looked back at the world of my childhood, it's curious to realize that it belonged more to the eighteenth than the nineteenth century. I can hear my father and Cabot Lodge talking about Jefferson as if he were an obnoxious neighbor of theirs. The Civil War was fresh in everyone's mind. My father had watched Lincoln's funeral procession. I can remember services on Memorial Day when nearly all the participants were *young* Civil War veterans. I had the feeling that the Revolution was not so far away and was very much aware of just how young a country we were.

We moved in a small and, I suppose, limited circle in Washington. There were people like Cabot Lodge and Henry Adams, Mr. Cameron, Mrs. Beale, the Tuckermans, etc. It was like living in a small university town. There were also a group of really old-timers known as the "cave dwellers." The Misses Riggs and Miss Patten and people like that.

Most of our friends lived on K Street and a few blocks to the north. The British Embassy was on Connecticut Avenue. We lived first on Jefferson Place. Cabot Lodge lived nearby. Georgetown was a separate world and going there something of an adventure.

The pace of life was leisurely. We would careen down Connecticut Avenue on our bikes from the top of the hill at Dupont Circle without encountering any traffic at all. I can remember the absolute consternation which was caused some years later when Mrs. Bob Taft collided with another car near Farragut Square. We had never seen or heard anything like it.

We used to go down and meet Father when he got off the streetcar at Farragut Square in the evening and walk home with him.

My stepmother became ill following Quentin's birth in 1897. This, coupled with the fact that, according to them, I was becoming unruly, made my family send me away to Auntie Bye's. Much as I adored her, I really didn't want to go. I was enjoying my freedom in Washington and had become a tomboy. My family said I was becoming a "guttersnipe" . . . not a good word to have hurled at one in those days.

I was the only girl in a boys' club and was frightfully pleased with myself. We met in a stable loft and the boys would come dressed in their sisters' clothes in order to deceive their parents. My father opened the door once on a petrified boy struggling to adjust one of his sister's dresses. They must have looked at each other with mutual consternation.

It was all harmless fun but viewed with some seriousness by my parents, especially because of my stepmother's illness. I was called very inconsiderate and sent away to New York on a day's notice. My brother Ted later joined me there.

The day after I arrived in New York, the *Maine* was blown up and two and one half months later my father was off to Cuba. My tomboyishness was quickly converted into a desire to become the Colonel of the Rough Riders, and, when that didn't materialize, I settled for the role of the colonel's daughter instead.

My father came to say good-bye to Ted and me before leaving.

Ethel, Ted, Kermit, and Alice with the Rough Riders in camp at Montauk Point. T.R. second from right and Bob Ferguson far left

Poor Father! He was so delighted to get into a war at last. We followed the progress of the Rough Riders avidly. And I made them improbable objects such as belly-bands for them to wrap around their middles in the tropics. When they returned in August, we were taken to their camp on Long Island to see the whole regiment on parade. It was an unforgettable sight.

My father took his Rough Riders' duties very seriously. He was always receiving letters from "comrades," usually detailing mishaps of one kind or another. There was one from a Rough Rider who had killed two men in Arizona and was "by all accounts entirely justified in the transaction." Another in Silver City was aiming at his wife when he apparently shot his sister-in-law instead.

Going from Oyster Bay to Albany when Father was made governor was anti-climactic. The Executive Mansion there was a hideous building with dreary dark furniture and a funereal air. Perhaps it has brightened now with lots of nice Rockefeller money.

The atmosphere of the town was pure Trollope. It even had a very Anglican bishop who wore gaiters, a three-cornered hat, and had a dog called Cluny.

We lived five blocks from the cathedral and we walked there on Sunday. We had to take an extra long way around if we misbehaved. The horses were never taken out on Sundays but we were allowed to take them sugar in the stable after lunch.

The communion tables in the Dutch Reformed Church where Father usually worshiped were placed in the middle of the aisle and one felt that any moment Peter Stuyvesant might appear.

One event I recall in Albany was having most of my teeth loosened when a girl in dancing class kicked me, unintentionally I suppose, in the jaw. I later developed abscesses and had to go to hospital in New York for quite awhile.

Two clashes with my parents occurred about this time. One was when I was told that I had to go to boarding school in New York. To Miss Spence's, which filled me with horror. I cried and carried on so successfully that after a couple of months the idea was dropped and I continued my lessons with my governess, Miss Young. Who was it who spoke of "the infinite capacity of the human brain to withstand the introduction of useful knowledge"? It echoes something once said by Hans Zinsser: "The tragedy of man is that he has developed an intelligence eager to uncover mysteries, but not sharp enough to penetrate them."

My confirmation also caused problems. The family said, "Now, darling. Here we are in Albany. You are fifteen and you ought to be confirmed." And I said, "No, I'm not going to be. Let me loose in your library instead." And they did.

My father's library was enchanting. He had an enormous variety of books, including many we were told not to read, such as *The Heart of Midlothian* (because it had an illegitimate child in it). Even some of Kipling's works were doctored for us for reasons I could never discover. To give my father credit, he detested sham, especially euphemisms like "enceinte" for pregnant and things like that. But he did have Principles.

Anything to do with sex or childbirth was just not discussed. Yet it was curious how much surreptitious attention was paid to the consequences of sex in those days. For instance, I never discussed such matters with my stepmother when I was a teenager, although she did come to me before I was married and said, "You know, before you were

Alice (back row right) doing theatricals in New York. 1898

born, your mother had to have a little something done in order to have you, so if you need anything let me know." It was couched in just those words. And I said, "Thank you very much." And that was that.

By the age of fifteen I knew quite a bit from the Bible and from my rabbits and guinea pigs. Living in the country as I did, you take these things for granted. They wouldn't admit that the Bible was a good place to learn the facts of life but I did just that.

However, when I tried to pass some of the information on to my cousin Eleanor, I almost came to grief. We were in the back bedroom at Auntie Bye's just after I had been "expelled" from Washington and I started imparting some of my newly found biblical knowledge . . . probably nothing more explosive than the "begat" series . . . when she suddenly leapt on me and tried to sit on my head and smother me with a pillow, saying I was being blasphemous. So I shut up and I think she probably went to her wedding not knowing anything about the subject at all. It was that kind of difference between us from the start.

Contraception was just never mentioned. I had a most wonderful German doctor, Dr. Sophie Nordhoff-Jung, and she knew a good deal on the subject, but most of my contemporaries were far too shy even to ask their doctors about such matters. I think most American doctors of the time would have been absolutely horrified, fearing lawsuits from irate husbands and things like that. But not dear Dr. Sophie. I still have a letter written to me shortly after I was married by my sister-in-law, Nan Wallingford, who was then the mother of three. In it she begged me to send her "one of those cunning labor-saving devices" so that she might save her "tottering reason."

T.R. took this picture of his daughter in the unlikely pose of a domes-ticated French peasant girl

White House Years

I suppose my first real interest in politics began with McKinley's election in 1896. There were no telephones in Sagamore in those days and I can still hear the crunch on the gravel outside as Uncle Jimmy Gracie drove up from the village in a buggy with a lantern on the back to tell us that Bryan had been beaten. For weeks before that, my brother Ted, who was then aged about eight, had given a series of speeches on Free Silver to the gardeners and to anyone else who would listen. He was the most active politician of us all at that age.

Later, when my father was nominated Vice-President, we were hideously annoyed. We wanted him as governor, not shoved into a sinecure by the moneyed interests and the party bosses such as Platt.[20] We thought he would be much better off as governor general of the Philippines instead.

I went up to Washington for McKinley's inauguration and watched the parade from a manicure shop on Pennsylvania Avenue. I remember going to the inaugural ball, which was held in the old Pension Office in those days. I was reproved for sitting on the arm of Mrs. McKinley's chair while she was in it. She was such a pathetic, frail little person. I hadn't even noticed she was there.

I was tremendously impressed by the sophistication of girls like Helen and Alice Hay, who made a point of wearing *old* dresses to the ball while I was trying to create an impression in excessively new white *point d'esprit* and a modest string of *jeune fille* pearls. At Albany, I had tried to make a similar effect by wearing a bridesmaid's dress I had from the wedding of my Uncle George Lee until it was virtually dropping off my back from overexposure. My stepmother suggested I donate it to the poor.

A portrait done in 1903

South view of the White House in 1904

Both Helen Hay and her sister Alice were good friends of mine. Helen was particularly attractive. She had one of those deep, husky voices and said pleasantly foolish things while eating a strawberry with one bite.

When we learned of McKinley's attempted assassination, we put on long faces and then my brother and I went outside and did a little jig. Then he rallied and a week later he died. By that time, I had gone to stay with some friends in the Adirondacks and had lost interest, had even become a little defiant about going to Washington. I remember feeling resentful when another girl told me how wonderful it was for me to be able to "come out" in the White House. I was overcome with shyness about the whole business of my father becoming President. I didn't even write to him and it was several weeks before I saw him again at Auntie Bye's in Farmington.

It's curious how fascinated people are about life in the White House. Certainly it was enchanting and interesting to be in that position, but we were never sanctimonious about it. We just thought of it as a house provided by the government for the man who happened to be President. Thank God they have stopped calling it the Executive Mansion.

The house was really rather ugly, inside at any rate. I have memories of hideous dark rooms and of Tiffany glass from the first time I was taken there to meet President Harrison as a child. My stepmother did quite a lot to renovate the place . . . or rather the firm of McKim and White did. They got rid of some of the more lugubrious touches such as the acres of plush and the overwrought gilt furniture. There were curtains in front of curtains in front of windows. There were a lot of heavy swags. It was what could only be described as late Grant and early Pullman. And there was a musty smell everywhere.

The layout was very simple. All the offices were where the bedrooms are now on the Treasury side. Everyone just went in the front door past a few stenographers and secretaries and you were right there.

The President's offices were on the same floor as the private rooms and were separated from them by a glass partition. There weren't anything like as many private apartments as there are today. The hall went right the way down the middle. Then there was a round room which was a library. Then the President's study. Then there was a big room, which was my parents' bedroom, and a dressing room. Opposite on the corner was another big room, which used to be my virginal bedroom. Now it is the private dining room. Ladybird Johnson told me it was much more convenient than going downstairs where the private dining room used to be. My sister Ethel had a small bedroom nearby and moved into mine when I got married. Ted's and Kermit's rooms were further up the hall. I think there were seven bedrooms in all.

Under the portico the two little boys and Mademoiselle held court. And that was all. There was a staircase at the end, which led down to the main hall. We used to slide down it on large tin trays from the pantry. Stilts and bicycles were allowed in the upstairs hall but not downstairs. We were forbidden the downstairs rooms when they were open to the public. Otherwise we pretty well had the run of the place. We loved it when the large potted palms sprouting out of the overstuffed circular seats in the East Room were removed and we could use the vacant spaces to launch surprise assaults on each other and anyone else who happened to be passing by.

McKim and White extended the dining room onto the terrace where there was an *enormous* conservatory, which was very Grant without the Pullman. I loved it there and so did a wonderful blue Brazilian macaw I had called Eli Yale.

The White House was very much more informal in those days. I can't actually remember my father going out and shaking hands with

The presidential bedroom. 1902

And Alice's

the tourists but he was available and large numbers poured in to see him. On occasions like New Year's Day crowds came in and I think he shook hands with all of them. They assembled outside just as if for a baseball game or a department store sale. They came in off the streets so to speak. It couldn't happen today.

There wasn't the same preoccupation with security as there is now. I think the Secret Service has grown in direct proportion to the interest of the press. My father had one Secret Service man, who went with him and who had to be able to ride. I remember one called Craig, who was killed when a trolley collided with the carriage in which he was traveling with my father. That must have been in 1902. I had seen him the day before as I was traveling in a train from Boston to Albany. It was an autumn sunset evening. Quite lovely. And as we passed slowly through a town, I looked out of the window and saw my father and Craig standing on the platform. I waved but they didn't see me.

The rest of the family didn't have any Secret Service protection. At least not when we first went to the White House. There was some-one who kept their eye on the two little boys. His name was Sloane, I think. He would get in the back of the cable car while they got in the

The East Room being restored

front. That kind of thing. But it was only off the grounds. We never saw them in the White House. Not when I was there anyway. My sister Ethel maintained she had to climb out of her bedroom window to avoid their surveillance, which strikes me as rather unnecessary. All she had to do was to make friends with them. The whole thing was very casual compared to what it is today.

I could always just take a walk and go down to old Bert's shoe shop on F Street and buy a pair of shoes without any difficulty. There was a village quality about Washington in those days and nobody bothered one. It was tremendously simple and easy.

The restrictions came more from the social conventions of the day. One was never allowed out with a date and one had to go to a dance with a chaperone. Lynda Johnson once asked me what I did for dates in the White House and I had to tell her there were no dates. One could never give a man a lift, not even a White House aide. There were always enough watchful eyes to check on one. Woe betide the girl who emerged from the conservatory at a dance with her hair slightly disheveled. As one's hair tended to fall down at the best of times it was frightfully difficult trying to keep up appearances.

I remember a friend of mine, who drove once from Bar Harbor to Ellsworth in Maine with a group of young people. Apparently when she left Bar Harbor she was wearing an embroidered dress buttoned up the back. When she arrived in Ellsworth, the buttons were askew. Consternation! I was told I wasn't to see her in certain houses after that. It was just like living in a village.

Entertaining in the White House was very simple. There were no chefs, just a cook. Caterers were used for the big events. I don't think we fed anyone at the receptions. That came later with the Tafts. We just had a selected group of about eighty for champagne and chicken sandwiches in the upstairs hall afterwards. Oh, the relief of those refreshments after standing around for several hours!

I don't remember much about the big dinners except that we sat at long tables rather than at the smaller ones they use today and that the table decorations could be quite elaborate. The Edwardians seem to have had a fetish for pink things and we were no exception. I have memories of lots of pink flowers . . . usually carnations and roses on the table . . . and pink shaded lights.

There were only seven embassies in Washington in those days. Or were there eight? Not more. Then there were a number of legations. Everyone knew everyone else. I remember a congressman coming to

Miss Alice Roosevelt

THE FIRST DEBUTANTE'S DANCE OF THE SEASON IN WASHINGTON

dinner at the White House and on arrival saying, "I couldn't bring the wife so I've brought my sister-in-law and two nieces instead." That sort of thing happened quite frequently. It had its funny side.

There were always a good assortment of guests at the White House. My father had a very wide range of interests and consequently attracted many different types of people. Of course there was nothing like the official state visits that there are today. No foreign kings and potentates. The nearest thing to one in my day was when Prince Henry of Prussia came over for the christening of the Kaiser's yacht, the *Meteor*, which was being built here. He was accompanied by a lot of German admirals, including Tirpitz. There hadn't really been a royal visit here since that of the Prince of Wales years before and Prince Henry's visit caused tremendous excitement in the press. I had to do the actual christening ceremony and felt tremendously pleased with myself. Broke a champagne bottle, hacked at a ribbon and mumbled a mercifully few words. I probably looked like one of those heavy-jawed Germanic princesses of the time who would wag a paw, nod a plumed hat and say, "I declare this bazaar . . . OPEN," to great bursts of applause.

In honor of the occasion the Kaiser gave me a bracelet with his miniature set in endearingly large diamonds (he gave me a similar one on my marriage but with much smaller diamonds). There were a number of other related festivities like a lunch on the *Hohenzollern* (the Kaiser's yacht on which Prince Henry had come over) and galas at the opera in

Launching the Kaiser's yacht, the Meteor. *1903*

New York. I enjoyed myself. I was only eighteen at the time and eating up the world.

The press reported everything. It's curious what an enormous interest there was in trivia. For instance a lot of fuss was made about a pet snake I had. I had called it Emily Spinach because it was as green as spinach and as thin as my Aunt Emily.[21] It was an affectionate, completely harmless creature, which I used to carry in a stocking box because it was a garter snake. Well, the stories multiplied about Emily Spinach until one would have thought that I was harboring a boa constrictor in the White House. Friends wouldn't allow me in their house with it and then finally one day I found it dead in its box. It had been killed (it was lying in a very unnatural position). I was so furious I couldn't see straight for weeks.

Then there was always a lot of interest in the press about our clothes. The smallest details were fluffed up and embellished. My stepmother and I didn't have many clothes . . . two or three evening dresses each perhaps. But to read the descriptions of our outfits in the papers you would think we lived at the dressmaker's. One report would describe how Mrs. Roosevelt had been in blue and silver with a diamond collar at one reception and in plain blue (minus the silver) and a lace bertha at another. The dress would be the same. Only the description was different.

I was lucky in that I had been a bridesmaid at quite a few weddings

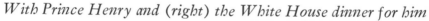

With Prince Henry and (right) the White House dinner for him

at that time and the dresses I wore had been altered and reworked until not even the sharpest columnist could keep track. Or if they did they were nice enough not to say so.

There hadn't been a girl in the White House . . . well, a grown-up one anyway . . . since Nellie Grant. So when they saw me, the daughter of a very popular President, I aroused some interest. There was no Hollywood and there were no movie stars in those days. They liked my father and there was I having a good time and not really giving a damn.

The whole attitude toward publicity was so ridiculous. I was brought up on the principle that "nice" people didn't get their names in the papers except when they were born, when they married, or when they died. We were always being enjoined not to talk to reporters and to avoid photographers. At the same time there was all this interest in our every move. The family were always telling me, "Beware of publicity!" And there was publicity hitting me in the face every day. It was unbelievable! And once stories got out, or were invented, I was accused of

Portraits taken at the White House in 1902 by Frances Johnston

Alice (second from left, center row) and Franklin Roosevelt (far right, front row) at a relative's wedding in 1904

courting publicity. I destroyed a savage letter on the subject from my father, because I was so furious with him. There was he, one of the greatest experts in publicity there ever was, accusing me of trying to steal his limelight.

At his inauguration, for instance, I was chided by him because I was waving to my friends and I said, "Well, you do it. Why shouldn't I?" And he said something to the effect of "But this is *my* inauguration." Bad blood right off!

The position of Presidents' families was pretty nebulous in those days. I recall my stepmother waxing very indignant about having her photograph taken. "Why do they want to photograph me?" she would say. "They only need a picture of the President." The loyal little wife always in the background!

Then imagine this. In those days a group of politicians would formally come to tell a candidate that he had been nominated for the presidency. It was all very civilized. Very formal. There would be more crunching of wheels on the gravel at Sagamore as a barouche full to top-hatted gentlemen would drive up. My father, also frock-coated and top-hatted, would be there to meet them. Hats would be lifted and smiles exchanged. Some kind of speech was made but we couldn't be sure what was said because where were we? Behind screen doors in the drawing room. My stepmother and I had to be hidden out of sight, like *houris* in the harem, while the men performed their stately minuet outside . . . tribal rites in which we had no part. It was extraordinary. At least *I* thought so. My stepmother accepted it as perfectly natural. I fantasized about what effect it would have if the screen doors flew open and the ladies of the harem tumbled out in a giggle. But it never happened. Pity.

We never had to do any campaigning as such. We were usually told just to keep out of the way and to sit behind the front row. Just before my father left the White House he found out that he was doing something at Lincoln's birthplace in Kentucky on the same day as I was laying a cornerstone in Ohio and he was very amused to think of me doing something in a public way.

Strangely enough, it was a little different when I was overseas. In places such as the Philippines and in Puerto Rico and Cuba I was called upon to fill a far greater number of public engagements. But not back here. I never had to speak in public, thank God! The mere thought of doing so has always turned me green with fright.

Although I did very much as I wanted, there were still quite a lot of restrictions. It wasn't very easy for me to entertain my friends in the White House for instance. There were only the Green and Red rooms and they were pretty public. If one wanted tea one had it in one's room. My stepmother was rather mean about things like that. Her sister Emily (after whom my snake was named) was one of those wizened virgins from birth. I can still hear my stepmother say when poor Aunt Emily requested tea, "If Miss Emily wants tea, she can have tea. In a thermos. In her room." I mean really!

So rather than sip from my thermos in my austere bedroom I would slip away to Auntie Bye's house. There one could have a good old English-style tea (with hot chocolate and champagne thrown in for good measure on Sundays) and meet all sorts of interesting people. My father often went there. He liked to meet people like Joe Cannon, who was the Speaker, there rather than in the more formal atmosphere of the White House.

"Uncle" Joe Cannon was quite a character. I sat next to him at my first official White House dinner. It was a few months before my

At the St. Louis Fair

coming-out party and I had been instructed to try and get the necessary funds out of him to have a hardwood floor laid in the East Room instead of having to put down "crash" over the existing muddy-colored carpet. I worked every ploy I knew on him, including Auntie Corinne's "elbow-in-the-soup" treatment, but to no avail. The floor was still unwooded when the dance took place in January. No alcohol was served either, much to my chagrin. I pleaded for just a little champagne, because that was the fashionable drink and I didn't want to be treated as a second-class citizen but my stepmother refused. I think my coming-out party was a hangover from the brownstone-front existence of my stepmother when they had *little* parties with a modicum of decorous dancing and an amusing fruit punch. The sort of parties Edith Wharton scoffed at.

My sister Ethel's coming-out some years later was very different. It was held in the Blue Room and was very lively and well organized and there were *buckets* of champagne. By that time I was married and I felt like a tottering ancient, but nevertheless managed to enjoy myself far more than I had at my own party.

My father never drank very much. Perhaps the example of Uncle Ellie was enough to temper him for life. He enjoyed champagne and a mixture of white wine and Apollinaris water, which was the White Rock of its day. He often used to drink from a large gold cup that he had been given when he visited San Francisco in 1905. It was made of Californian gold. He loved it and he always had it when champagne was served. People would say that he had a metal cup so that nobody would know how much he drank. The rumors then started that he was an old soak. It was incredible.

I really didn't have many friends of my own age when I was young. I mean, I knew a lot of people but only saw the ones who interested me, and they were usually five or ten years older than I. The ones of my own age were busy dancing with little boys from Groton, St. Paul's and St. Mark's or slightly bigger ones from Harvard and Yale. All that bored me. Also it was before deodorants and being clutched in one's partner's arms and whirled around a stifling room could be a heady experience. They were frightfully nice and proper and respectable but they were not terribly interesting. I always liked older men. A father complex coming out, presumably. I didn't particularly like boys. They were all over the place when I came out but there was I, one of those dear little virgins giving the older ones a good time. I was amused by them but I wasn't very sexy about them. I tended to regard questions of sex with a certain amount of mirth. Attraction for me had very little to do with sex. It was more closely connected with a certain vitality, a sense of humor, and a mental affinity. That was when the mayhem started.

My father was always taking me to task for gallivanting with "society" and for not knowing more people like my cousin Eleanor. Poor Father! Most of these society friends were the offspring of his own childhood friends, whom he had spurned. He was very self-conscious about it. Auntie Bye wasn't like that at all. She had a tremendously good time with everyone. So did Auntie Corinne. I think he felt he was betraying the high principles of his own father, who was very much a do-gooder. They used to feed newsboys at Christmas. That kind of thing. A pat of butter and a pound of cheese. All *that*.

He liked certain social figures. Grace Vanderbilt, for instance, perhaps because she was pretty and feminine and appeared so helpless. Everything was a fairy story for her. There she was, the pretty Southern belle, queen of society, married to a Vanderbilt; she seemed to sail along on a wave of fantasy. She *adored* royalty and her yacht was named the *Kingfisher*. Tragedy never seemed to strike. I see her now

Her sister Ethel *With Eli Yale, her pet macaw*

Standing on the parapet at Grace Vanderbilt's house in Newport

with an enormous stomacher of diamonds pouring down her front like "the waters coming down at Lahore" and a tiara crammed into one of those incredible lamé bandeaux she used to wear in later life. She was never quite sure whether the joke was at her expense or not. She once gave me what she probably thought was an affectionate nibble on the ear and I gave her my bull ape imitation and let out such a howl of rage that she ran from the room screaming.

Father scorned bluestockings like Mrs. Cadwalader Jones and her sister-in-law Edith Wharton, who were both good friends of mine and my stepmother's. Mrs. Cadwalader Jones gave me my first volume of the *Oxford Book of English Verse*, which has traveled round the world with me ever since.

He tended to hide his feelings about women, however. He had been in Sweden once and when he came back he said, "That dull, second-rate court." Apparently they were pretty dreadful but among

Grace Vanderbilt wearing a good many diamonds

In New York. 1905

Riding at the White House. 1902

them was the Russian Grand Duchess Marie, who was married to a Swedish prince, and he found her absolutely delightful and charming. She obviously enjoyed meeting my father and they had a good time together. I teased him about this and he said, "Alicy, don't forget I'm human." Poor darling! That's as near as he could admit to a liking for female company. It was all so Victorian. I remember him saying about the Greeks, "Wonderful people, but for their attitude to women." About their attitude to men I don't think he would have had the vaguest notion. Was it George V who is reported to have said about a peer arrested for homosexuality, "I thought men like that shot themselves"? Well, Father was a bit like that. I wonder what he would have made of a letter I received from one of the Gay Liberation groups offering to make me their first Honorary Homosexual. He would have been more than mystified. I've always been a supporter of people's sexual rights "as long as they don't do it in the street and frighten the horses" as Mrs. Patrick Campbell said. Who knows, perhaps homosexuality is nature's way of keeping the population down? At least it is one of the best natural remedies we could possibly have, and if it keeps them happy and pleased, why not?

It was my father's attitude to Large Families, the Purity of Womanhood, and the Sanctity of Marriage which humiliated, shamed and embarrassed me. I mean, have you ever read what was called his Race Suicide letter? It was addressed to a lady in Philadelphia and was given great publicity at the time.[22] Its sentiments are absolutely outrageous and it was to protest what I considered the *indecent* behavior of my father in this matter that I founded something called the Race Suicide Club. There were four founding members. The other three were rather older friends. I was eighteen, they about twenty-four. I can still see these three elderly, quivering virgins creeping out onto the back portico of the White House where we held our secret meetings. They were all basically prim and the idea that there might be anything even remotely pleasurable in sex was *unthinkable*. So I devised something called the Golden Token, which went with several commandments. I think I still have a copy of them somewhere. I wish I could remember the exact words. They went something like this:

Question: "What would thou then submit to in return for the Golden Token?"
Answer: "I will submit to all but the token will not be forthcoming."

I made them recite it and they were absolutely *terrified* because they thought someone might be listening or that we were being bugged. There we were making the rudest game of my father, who would not have been at all amused if he had known.

Thank God the Race Suicide Club was not unmasked. Coming on top of my other eccentricities, it might have proved the final straw. Driving a car alone and smoking in public were bad enough. Then there was the time that I was seen paying money to a bookie at the races and they said that would probably wreck my father's chances of re-election, so that was all hushed up. It was all so harmless it was pathetic. I was just having a good time. Protesting a bit, I suppose, but I was pretty much alone in doing so. The Lonely Libber.

"Alice, Where Art Thou?"

My so-called "goings-on" met with a lot of antagonism from groups such as the Woman's Christian Temperance Union, who kept on writing to my father protesting how he could possibly permit his daughter to become a scarlet woman. Carry Nation and I were said to be at loggerheads. Then the family asked me not to smoke under their roof and I was smoking on top of it (the roof was about the only place one could escape to in the White House in those days). Frightfully annoying for the poor things but they were very good about it. Both of them.

It was to Owen Wister, who wrote *The Virginian*, that my father made the remark that he could either run the country or he could control me but that he couldn't possibly do both. It was prompted by the fact that I had waltzed into his office with Emily Spinach on my arm or something. It was said very mirthfully.

Because of restrictions in Washington, I did a lot of escaping to other parts of the country . . . to New Orleans for carnival, to Kansas City and St. Louis, and to Chicago for the Horse Show. A cartoon captioned "Alice, Where Art Thou?" beautifully captured the mob scene on my arrival there. I found it very exciting because I was amused by it all.

I was invited to go to Edward VII's coronation in 1902 but the press got very silly about that and started wondering whether my aunts were going to be my ladies-in-waiting. There were other protocol problems, which apparently got so involved that my father asked me not to go and suggested that I visit Cuba instead.

It was my first visit to the tropics. Cuba was still very Spanish colonial in atmosphere. I stayed in Havana in the palace of the old governors general with General and Mrs. Wood. There were lots of entertainments and sightseeing. We used to drive round the Prado in the evening with me holding my breath each time we passed the local leper asylum. I had a childish fear about leprosy, which took years to overcome.

The trip to the Far East in 1905 was by far the most exciting one I ever made. We first went to Japan, which was "*banzai, banzai, banzai*" all the way. It was just before my father concluded the Treaty of Portsmouth, which ended the Russo-Japanese War, and the Japanese were obviously hoping for great things. They didn't get them, and we were received very differently when we went back a few months later.

In Japan. 1905

Not a *banzai* to be heard and I was told to say I was English if asked my nationality.

We lunched with the Emperor Meiji on the first visit. They sat on one side of the table. We sat on the other. The Emperor didn't make much impression on me, but then we only managed small talk through interpreters. The Empress never appeared, but she sent me an embroidered screen and a lacquer box and a photograph of herself dressed up in European evening dress. Apparently they used to order everything package deal from Paris. Tiara, parure, dresses, the lot. Can't you just see her scribbling off a letter, "Dear Mr. Worth, please send me one complete Empress's outfit."

There was also rather a grand garden party for us at the American Legation. All the Japanese ladies wore big floppy hats and carried parasols. I have some photographs of that. We look like a slightly stoned version of the Ascot scene from *My Fair Lady*.

The trip to China came later, after we had been in the Philippines. Only a small party of us went. The main group with Secretary Taft went back from Hong Kong. We went by steamer and train to Peking, where we were met by a posse of court officials. Most of them had been at Harvard or Oxford and spoke impeccable English. One had even been the cox of the Cambridge rowing crew.

The Dowager Empress was at the Summer Palace and we went there to stay the night before being "received." We were lodged in Prince Ch'ing's quarters. I had a whole hall to myself. The place seemed immense, an endless succession of courtyards and pavilions.

They gave us a huge dinner the first night. The courses alternated between "European" food, which was served with champagne, and Chinese dishes with which we had a delicious local rose wine, like a brandy and *very* strong. I didn't like the champagne but loved the other. The result was I got quite drunk. I remember saying in carefully enunciated tones, "Good night, Mabel, good night, Mrs. Newlands,"[23] and thinking, "Am I able to walk that line without swaying?" as I wove my way off to bed. I didn't even notice my hard Chinese pillow that night and must have fallen asleep in my evening clothes because I can remember getting up in the early hours of the morning and hurriedly putting on my nightgown before being roused by my maid Anna, who would have been absolutely horrified if she had found me fully clothed in a stupor. She was one of those *very* sour, frightfully superior beings (an American, which was novel, as most people had for-

En route to the Far East

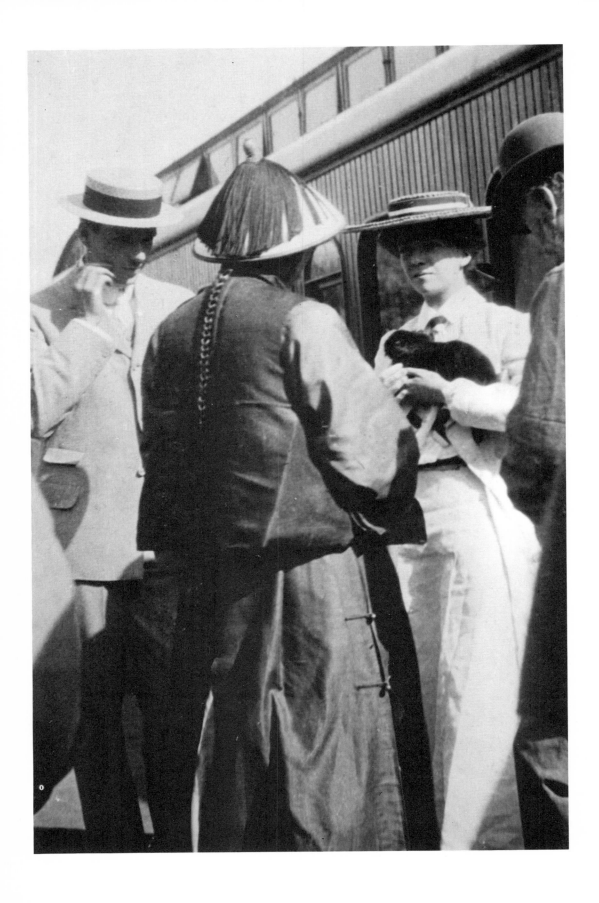

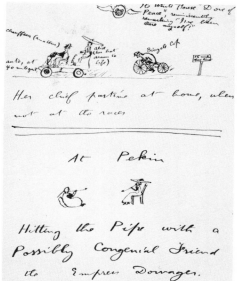

A contemporary rendering of the scene (left) and a letter from T.R. to his daughter in China

eign maids then); and I think she must have *hated* the whole trip. She almost had a nervous breakdown in the Philippines and had to be sent away for a little "rest and recuperation."

The audience with the Dowager Empress took place at eight in the morning so I barely had time to struggle into my clothes before being escorted to the ceremony. Luckily I had been a bridesmaid three or four times that year so I had a number of pretty outfits available and didn't have to waste time planning what I was going to wear on occasions of this kind.

Before going into the audience hall we were taken into a small room which had a basin, scent, soap but no water, so there was no chance to have a final cleanup and we were only able to douse ourselves with scent before going in.

The audience hall seemed rather large as I steered myself, still feeling slightly unsteady on my feet, toward the throne, making the obligatory three curtsies as I went forward in stages. The Empress was seated on what I suppose was her "Dragon Throne," very erect and looking just like her picture. Piercing, alert black eyes and a rather cruel, thin mouth, which turned up at one corner and drooped at the other. She

Leaving Peking with Manchu in her arms

大清國當今聖母皇太后萬歲萬歲萬萬歲

光緒癸卯年

The Dowager Empress of China

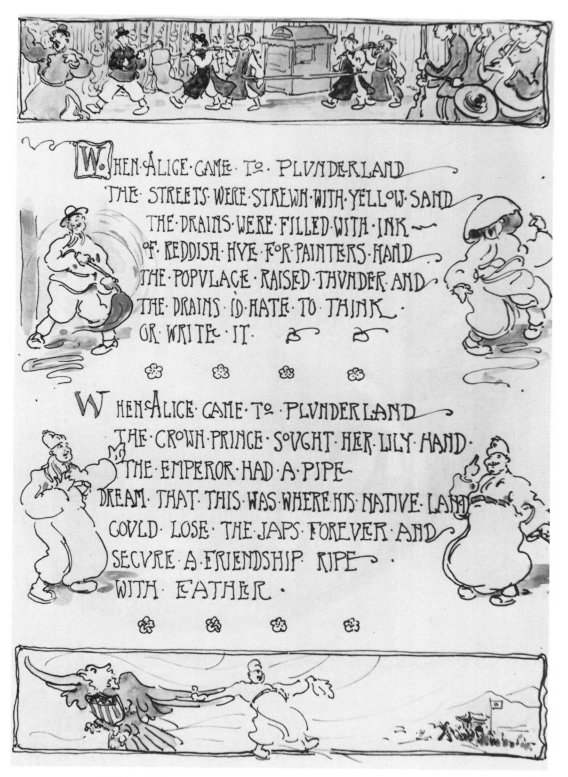

When Alice came to Plunderland
The streets were strewn with yellow sand
The drains were filled with ink—
Of reddish hue for painters hand
The populace raised thunder and
The drains id hate to think·
Or write·it·

When Alice came to Plunderland
The crown prince sought her lily hand·
The emperor had a pipe
Dream·that·this·was·where his native land
Could·lose·the japs·forever·and
Secure·a·friendship·ripe·
With·father·

Willard Straight's poem entitled Alice in Plunderland

(Left) Leaving for the Imperial Palace, Tokyo and with Taft on arrival at Yokohama

At a garden party in the American Legation, Tokyo

wore a loose, heavily embroidered Chinese coat and a brocade skirt and her hair was carefully brushed back into one of those Manchu headdresses made of trembling pearls, jade, and artificial flowers. She was byzantine-looking only in the sense that she seemed so rigid in her clothes.

The Emperor (Kuang-hsü), who was her nephew, I think, sat on one of the bottom steps of the throne, but nobody paid any attention to him. He just sat there all huddled and staring around rather vacantly, poor thing. She had already done away with one heir to the throne (her son, T'ung-chih) and she got rid of this one shortly afterwards as well.

The audience didn't last too long and then we were taken off to have lunch with the so-called Empresses of the East and the West, who were the Emperor's two principal wives. It was a merry meal because there were no interpreters, so we just chatted away at each other in our own languages, with neither side understanding a word.

Then we went out into the palace gardens, where we were joined

With the wives of American diplomats

And the Japanese Minister of War

At a sumo wrestling match

In the Philippines

by the Dowager Empress, who was followed by a number of attendants bearing gifts. I've forgotten what exactly I got. Gold bracelets (set with rather inferior rubies), rings (lost those), jade and pearl earrings (still have those), some of those extraordinary long nail sheaths which they used to wear (I later made them into a brooch), and of course bolts and bolts of brocade. She was certainly very generous with her presents, but then the Chinese always were. And I absolutely loved all the loot I amassed. My family used to say it would have to be a nailed-down, red-hot stove for me not to carry it off. I returned from the Far East laden with booty and, much to my chagrin, my father made me pay duty on *all* of it. A great friend of mine, Willard Straight,[24] who used to be with our legation in Korea, wrote a poem about all the presents I collected on this trip. It was called *Alice in Plunderland*. Heavenly title!

A revealing incident occurred when I was talking with the Dowager Empress in the garden. Our conversation was conducted through an interpreter, a gentleman called Wu T'ing-fang who had been the Chinese Minister in Washington and who was someone whom we had known and liked and often had to the White House. He began interpreting, standing between us, but suddenly the Empress said something very sharply to him. The poor man turned quite ashen, dropped on all fours, and kept his forehead stuck to the ground, only lifting it briefly to translate. I have often wondered why she made such a point of deliberately humiliating him before us. I discussed it later with my father and we decided that it was to show us that a man, whom we accepted as an equal, was no more than a lackey she could put her foot on. She was very much the Red Queen in many ways. And of course one must remember that this was just after the Boxer Rebellion and I

think that, despite all the social courtesies we were shown, they really *hated* us.

The Dowager Empress left shortly after this incident and we went on to tour the gardens. The rest of the group went on foot, but I was given a magnificent yellow-tasseled sedan chair with eight bearers. We must have looked an amusing sight as we trotted along, I borne aloft, still all hatted and white-gloved, surrounded by a chattering group of court officials and eunuchs. The head eunuch had the wonderful nickname of Cobbler's Wax. We ended up in a vast marble summerhouse, built in imitation of a Chinese junk, on the palace lake and were treated to tea, sweetmeats, and very, very old eggs.

Next day more presents were sent to me at the legation. Two minor officials brought a beautiful small black Pekingese on a cushion, followed shortly afterwards by a high official and an imperial sedan chair, escorted by a whole troop of cavalry, which contained nothing but a framed photograph of the Empress.

I had the dog for several years. I called it, most originally, Manchu. It was an affectionate creature, despite the fact that it had been emasculated . . . no, that's the wrong word because it was a she . . . but it had, you know, been *dealt with*. They wouldn't have dreamt of giving a foreigner a dog who could breed. Curious animal. I once saw it dancing on its hind legs in the moonlight on the White House lawn. Some mysterious ancestral rite perhaps?

From Peking we went to Tientsin to dine with General Yuan Shih-kai, who was then the viceroy of Chihli and a tremendously powerful figure in China at that time. We had another of those huge Chinese dinners and this one was complicated by the fact that his wife had the notion that to be a perfect hostess she must first take the food on

With Taft in the Philippines

On board the Manchuria. *A fancy dress party with Taft in the center, Alice directly in front of him*

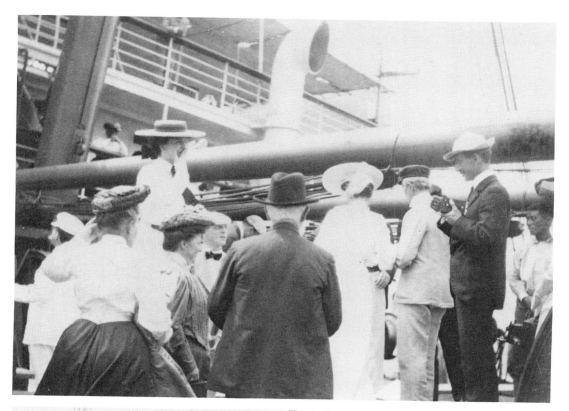

The Empress of Japan

In Hawaii

At the American Legation in Korea. Nicholas Longworth seated on the ground, right. Willard Straight fourth from right

her plate, taste it, and then put it on mine. Luckily, he rather sternly put a stop to this practice.

We couldn't go to Canton because of strong anti-foreigner sentiment there. But I was given a wonderful poster by the consul there, which I still have. It is a cartoon of me being carried in a sedan chair by tortoises, which was apparently the ultimate insult. The Chinese government were said to be outraged by the insult but I found it hilarious.

Korea was something of an anticlimax after China. We sailed to Chemulpo and then went by special train to Seoul. The streets were very crowded and were lined with the imperial bodyguard and we were carried from the station to the legation in sedan chairs, escorted by men carrying lanterns on long poles. But somehow it was all slightly sad and pathetic. Everyone was dressed in rather dirty white—in mourning for their Empress—and they looked so downtrodden. The country was beginning to slip into Japanese hands and I must say that the Japanese army officers I saw looked *exceptionally* smart and competent.

The legation was just next door to the Imperial Palace and one could see the little Emperor, or a little something, peeking through the

The anti-American poster in Canton

curtains to see what was happening on our side of the fence. We went to lunch with him; and, there again, it was all a little pathetic. He was a sad-looking man, wearing lots of lovely, fluttery little garments. Not grand at all. When we went in to lunch, he positively hung onto my arm. I didn't have his. He had mine. And then afterwards the only presents he could find to give me were the lacquer plates we had eaten off.

I enjoyed these trips tremendously. I valued my independence from an early age and was always something of an individualist. Well, a show-off anyway. One of the only things I remember about the *Forsyte Saga* was when the little dog comes in and wanders around. Nobody pays any attention to it. It goes to the middle of the floor and throws up, so the lady calls the butler to take it away and to wipe up the mess. As he leaves the room the butler says, "The little animal likes to make itself felt, madam." Well, a great deal of that kind of thing goes on in other spheres.

I suppose a lot of my showing off was a defense against the incipient shyness which almost everyone has. And, being the offspring of a very conspicuous parent, I wasn't going to let him get the better of me.

Without wanting to go too deeply into it, I think it is true to say

T.R. on tour

that my father didn't want me to be a burden . . . a guilty burden . . . on my stepmother. He obviously felt guilty about it, otherwise he would have said at least once that I had another parent. The curious thing is that he never seemed to realize that *I* was perfectly aware of it and developing a resentment. I had a great affection for him but tended to worship from afar. I don't think he had any special affection for me. I think he certainly did for my sister Ethel, and for Quentin because he was the youngest and he was killed. He was so young and my father was old and crippled then and still living. That sort of feeling.

I used to tease him and say, "Look at you. Six children. Five splendid torchbearers and one will-o'-the-wisp, not one going round bleating about nobility and purity and the sanctity of womanhood." We enjoyed teasing each other. And arguing. With me usually doing so from the opposite point of view from the one I believed in order to be provocative.

We used to talk over a lot of things at breakfast when I was young. Father always used to be in the best of spirits then and we discussed everything under the sun. Well, almost. We usually had breakfast about eight-thirty and it would be a proper English-type

Ditto Alice

breakfast, not just hominy and grits. The only awful part was having to kiss Father. One tried to aim somewhere on his face but his mustache usually got in the way. He never hung it out to dry and it was invariably wet and smelling of shaving soap in the morning. The boys got away with just a "good morning" but Ethel and I had to do the kissing part. She was small and docile and didn't mind. I minded terribly.

When I look back on it now, which I rarely do, I can feel a little mean about my father, especially as a politician rather than as a person. The eyebrows tend to lift and the canines to show. He was certainly fine for the period he lived in. Absolutely perfect. It was a time when we needed large families and armies and expansion overseas. It was all in the great imperial tradition. But I tend to see it through the eyes of young people today and one just can't have a prayerful attitude to it all.

I mean, just look at his desire to go and fight in a war. Any war. He wanted to go and fight for the Chileans at one time. Or was it the Peruvians? Cabot Lodge and his friends used to tease him about that and call him the "Chilean Volunteer" and say "Really, Theodore, how ridiculous!" It was quite an obsession with him. Then the Cuban expedition came along and provided him with exactly what he was looking for. It was perfect timing.

I think that much of his militarism came from the fact that his father, whom he adored, had not fought in the Civil War but had bought a substitute instead. With a heavily Southern wife, perhaps there was no alternative. He certainly didn't spare himself in the war. He was on the Allotments Commission and went out in the most awful weather to give the troops their allotments but the fact remains that he never saw active service and my father never forgot that. I could always make him angry by saying about Lincoln, his great hero, "How do you account for Lincoln writing that letter to Grant, saying that his son needed a job on his staff? He wanted him to see a little bit of the war." That was very hard on Father.

When he wanted to raise a division in the First World War, the idea was put forward that it could be under a Canadian flag. He liked the idea and said he would put a bison in the corner. We said a dodo would be more appropriate. Poor Father! He really wanted that division. He told Wilson, "Anything that has gone before will be as dust in a windy street, Mr. President, if you will let me have this division."

I went with him to the White House that day and afterwards we took a drive. The division was the one thing he wanted. He wanted that opportunity and it was a very bitter thing when it was refused.

T.R. going over the top

I only wish he hadn't become somewhat swamped by his *Boys' Own Paper* image, because there was another side to him. He had an enormous range of interests and enthusiasms, many of which he shared with us. He was enchanting that way. He had a great knowledge and love of books, although he was not really an intellectual. I can see him now hunched near a lamp with a book held very close to his head in order to read better. His eyesight was always poor and for the last ten years of his life he was virtually blind in one eye, a fact that very few people realized.

He spent a good deal of time with us, and not just in rowdy games. When we were older he often consulted with us. I remember when he was writing a speech once which he was due to give at Madison Square Garden, he would pass over the first draft of every sheet to me as he finished writing it. There were no speech writers in those days. Or at least he never used them. He just did it as a matter of course because we were good friends.

Although he had a great knowledge of books, he wasn't much of an art lover. "Obviously mammalian but not necessarily human" was his comment on seeing the famous picture of the "Nude Descending the Staircase" at the Armory Show in 1913. He could be funny about things like that, although the fact that he was also extremely near-sighted might have accounted for that particular remark. On another occasion he said of a statue that it was an exceptionally fine Diana when in actual fact it was of Apollo.

He had a melancholic streak which didn't come out very often but which was noticeable when it did. It ran in his family, I think. We all had it to one degree or another. I don't have it so much because I recognize it. But Father's was very real. Very fatalistic. He thought for instance that the vice-presidency was the end of his career and he was very depressed about that. Wondered whether he could practice law while in office. My stepmother had a very calming influence on him, especially when he was in an excitable mood. He used to walk around the garden with her for at least an hour every morning. I can't imagine a President being able to do that today.

He had a rather simple religious faith unencumbered by philosophical niceties. He taught Sunday school in college. That kind of thing. He believed rather strongly in certain elementary principles and moral values. He could be quite tough about mistresses and illegitimate babies and all that. Very Mr. Gladstone, although he wasn't one of his most ardent admirers. He didn't approve of Gladstone's nocturnal jaunts to rescue fallen women. He felt that wasn't quite nice.

He was one of the earliest conservationists. This was a genuine feeling and not a political ploy. I think it was one of the greatest legacies he left, although he suffered from being a pioneer in the field. He and Gifford Pinchot[25] really started conservation in this country. Pinchot was a charming, wonderful character, slightly younger than my father, and a close family friend. We used to call him The Forester. He was very appealing to the ladies and even my spinster Aunt Emily believed for a time that he was intended for her and had to be disabused of this notion. I am reminded of that wonderful line of E. A. Robinson's, "The patient ardour of the unpursued."

When one comes to think of it, we were tremendously sectionalized in those days. A politician in, say, New York might know what was going on in the Midwest but almost certainly not in the Far West. The fact that my father had lived for quite a while in the Dakotas and knew the territory well set him apart. He had a real *feeling* for the West. You must remember that those were still pioneer days. It's hard to believe that the Indian uprising occurred when he was at the Dakota ranch and that there were cattle thieves in his back yard.

He saw the population increasing and the interests in oil development and what have you destroying some of the country and he was concerned. He was very genuinely for the public interest.

I think the quality of men serving in my father's administration was pretty high. Maybe I'm just seeing it from the perspective of age but I don't think so. Men like Elihu Root and Philander Knox and of course John Hay,[26] who was certainly the outstanding member of the Cabinet. In my father's day the Cabinet tended to be a bit like Christ and the apostles. It was terribly respectable and respected. Now nobody knows who is in the Cabinet. To begin with, it has grown enormously. And my father kept things in line. He just didn't allow nasty things to happen. For instance, he told John King, who was a politician in Connecticut and a great supporter of his, "You provide the politics and I'll provide the morals." It is true that King got out of line but only after my father had left office.

Cabot Lodge loomed large in our lives. I remember him from earliest childhood. We used to call him "Pinky" and he had a charming wife called Nanny. Cabot always had a slight feline quality. He purred with just the faintest suspicion of a snarl. And he had a quality of detached intellectual superiority, which some found rather disconcerting. The Boston Brahmin bit. He came from people who had read books for generations and he was hideously aware of it. He was the type of person who knew exactly what to laugh at and what not to. Spontaneity was not one of his virtues. Actually there was not much of a premium put on intellect in those days. To some it was considered rather suspect.

I can't understand the fascination there seems to be about the Edwardian world today. I for one don't look back on it with any particular nostalgia. To me it is a curious, faraway world, which in many respects is closer to the eighteenth century than life today. It was certainly a leisurely existence. Everything was slow. Going to Europe then was a major event and took months. "Society" went and arranged itself for the season, bought clothes in Paris, came trotting back, perhaps went up the river for a brief moment, then to Newport, perhaps up the river again, New York for Christmas, worried through the winter, and then it was time to go to Paris again for more clothes and on to London. It was rather like living in a perpetual Christmas play.

There was a terrible self-consciousness of Americans at that time about the British. They adored and *aped* everything British. It was a time when all those young (and sometimes not so young) American heiresses were leaping across the Atlantic to marry European aristocracy. I recall a lovely Charles Dana Gibson cartoon about the social lend lease of the day, which perfectly captures the spirit of it.

It was extraordinary how quickly these ladies became assimilated into the English social scene after they were married. They even managed that curious fluffed-up way of talking of the English upper classes of that time.

I had a friend, Beatrice Granard, who was very much the English grande dame. She was married to Lord Granard, who was Master of the Horse. And twitched. I stayed with her once at the delightful house her parents had in Paris. She said to me one day in her lispy "Mayfair" accent, "Do you want to come shopping with me this afternoon, Alice? "Sweet (her father) has promised to buy me a tiara for little dinners. But don't tell Twin or he will have to buy her one too." Twin was her younger sister. A tiara for *little* dinners. I ask you! Heaven knows what she had for the big ones.

Beatrice and Twin were pure-bred American girls. Their father, Ogden Mills, had inherited lots of California gold rush money and their mother, Tiny Livingston, was descended from one of the signers of

*Charles Dana Gibson's cartoon about the American girl abroad "chaper-
oned by a real Duchess, with two noblemen ready to marry her, and yet
her happiness is not complete."*

the Declaration of Independence. They were very grand and lived in a
"stately home" on the Hudson, which became even statelier with the
advent of the forty-niner money and stretched, much larger than the
White House, down to the river.

I once asked Beatrice's mother what she had given her daughter as
a wedding present and she said, with a vague wave of her hand, "Oh,
she took a *parure*." As if they were lying around the house for the asking. Along with the tiaras.

A lot of what Noel Coward used to call "tumbril talk" went on in
those days. Tumbril talk is what rich and/or aristocratic folk might say
on the way to the guillotine. It usually reflects a rather startling una-
wareness about how anyone else lives. Marie Antoinette was reputed to
be very good at it.

A good example of tumbril talk is when an extremely wealthy
New York lady, who had never ridden on a bus, decided to do so and
got on one to ride down Fifth Avenue. It was the days when the con-
ductor came around and collected the fares in a small bag. When he
came to her she smiled brightly and said, "Oh no, my good man. You
see, I have my own charities I contribute to."

There was lots of tumbril talk at the Millses'. I can hear Tiny saying to her husband, "Ogden, why do you bother about going into politics? You see very unattractive people there. You could look after your family affairs. That's quite enough to do, don't you think?" They had a delicious sense of their own importance.

Nancy Astor, who was a good friend of mine, was a frightful show-off but if you called her bluff she could be fun. She was not really given to tumbril talk but she did have a somewhat zany and very caustic wit. Her sisters were enchanting. There was an elder one called Liz, who had grown up before they left Richmond and became county, and then there was a very attractive one called Irene, who was engaged to Nick when she was about fifteen. She later married Charles Dana Gibson and became the Gibson Girl. The only person I knew who could really control Nancy was her husband, Waldorf. I remember at the Black Derby of 1910 just after Edward VII had died, when everyone, even the gypsies, wore black, Nancy was going on about how the rival jockey who had won had cheated. She said everything she could possibly say and then Waldorf very quietly turned to her and said, "If I hear another word I shall withdraw all our horses from the track for the rest of the season." She shut up like a clam.

Nancy had been converted to Christian Science by Mrs. Henry Bull, whose husband had been a Rough Rider. I made a remark to her once about how relatively easy it must be to switch Blessed Marys in midstream and she wasn't terribly amused.

I also associate the 1910 Derby with suffragettes throwing themselves under horses and chaining themselves to railings. They were glorious. There were all those enchanting British ladies. One moment they would be all charm and gentleness, the next they would be throwing themselves under horses and tying themselves to trees. It was wonderful.

I saw quite a lot of Jennie Jerome[27] about this time. Later in life she tended to cling to anyone who reminded her of her American past. She was really rather miserable with her later marriages.

When Winston Churchill first came here during the Spanish-American War I think he was rather ashamed of his American background. He wouldn't have minded if Spain had won in Cuba, I believe . . . the proud old monarchy with the great imperial tradition. All that.

My father and Churchill did not get on very well. He said Churchill was bad-mannered, didn't get up when ladies came into the room, and things like that, but I think that it was really more due to the fact that

deep down they were perhaps both working the same side of the street. They were very alike in many respects. They were both activists, enormously productive, vigorous, loved the English language and history . . . not to mention histrionics. I think that my father was the more widely read of the two but Churchill was always a great orator. He had learned a lot in this respect from Bourke Cockran,[28] with whom he used to stay when he first came over here.

Bourke was an old family friend. I seem to have known him forever. I remember him coming into the room at Auntie Bye's when I was a child just as I had lost one of my first teeth in a piece of spongy cake and was trying to find it. Later he came on the trip to the Far East and fell in love and later married Anne Ide, the daughter of the then Vice-Governor of the Philippines. She and her sister were both extraordinarily beautiful and were just enough ravaged by being so long in the tropics to be exquisitely pale and interesting. Bourke, in contrast, was not at all physically attractive but he had enormous charm and was very amusing. He had a most delightful Irish voice, and although his sympathies were Irish, he was also very pro-English. "You are an Anglophobe in public and an Anglomaniac in private," I used to tell him.

Oh, those Edwardian beauties! They rise before me with their large bosoms compressed in strange ways. They were flattened out with straight corsets in front and then their backsides were pushed out into great big tails behind. Extraordinary!

I have visions of Mrs. Keppel, who was Edward VII's great friend and a most imposing Edwardian figure, going round the garden of her Florentine villa and saying imperiously to her gardener with a wave of her parasol, "Bisognia begonia."

I had as little to do with that look as possible. Certainly I never wore any of the carapaces and other items of harness which seemed to be *de rigueur* . . . I use the word advisedly . . . for so many.

I was always trying to take away rather than to add to the ribbons, flounces, and furbelows one had to wear in those days. I wasn't really very interested in dress. I just liked well-made things, which were essentially simple in style. I had . . . still have . . . a weakness for beautiful fabrics. I relished for years the exquisite brocades I was given in China. But I dislike fussy things and there were plenty of those in the Edwardian period. The hats could be outrageous . . . great cartwheels loaded down with fruit, flowers, feathers, ribbons, and dead birds. Gradually I was able to strip them all off and was left with something very basic. Until she died a few years ago a local milliner used to make the same hats for me in three different shades . . . black, blue, and brown. They were made of felt in winter, straw in summer. They were replaced only when they got worn and fell off my head. They got a nice patina with wear.

The original Alice-blue garment I had was actually a wrapper, not a dress. It faded like mad and patches of a sort of turquoise blue had to be put in to keep it afloat. I didn't see the show (*Irene*), which started the whole silly publicity about it, but when the revival came here a few years ago, the promotion man kept on calling me up and saying things like, "Darling, I like you so much for having a good time." Too awful! But if I had been nasty to him it would have been like hitting a blind lamb on the nose.

I didn't really have many clothes when I was young although the press pretended I did. When I went on the trip to the Far East the details of my hatboxes and the box for my sidesaddle, etc., were listed in breathless detail, although that was considered a perfectly normal way to travel in those days. The hatboxes were wonderfully designed so that you could pin the hats around the sides and not crush them. Anna, who was my personal maid, used to try and keep me as uncrumpled as possible but it was not always easy. Before the advent of dry cleaning one needed a whole battery of instruments and strange devices to keep all those ruffles and bows looking spry.

It wasn't only dress that was restricting in those days. There was an incredible overlay of formality to social life generally. Etiquette could be a minefield but I never paid much attention to that. But oh, those little notes asking one about cotillions and thanking you for having done . . . or not done . . . this and that. My poor stepmother had a long-suffering secretary called Belle Hagner who wrote most of mine for me. I still have a plaintive note from her, asking me what I wanted done with a pet monkey, which someone had sent me from heaven knows where. There was a lot of that, especially around the time of my wedding. I suppose it is a great failing but I just never developed a feeling for writing letters. I never found it the best way to communicate and the telephone made it unnecessary to a great extent.

The other thing I hated was "calling," whereby on a certain set day each week one was meant to leave one's visiting card on various worthies. I just refused to do it. It seemed such a pointless waste of time.

Marriage and Aftermath

My wedding would have been at Sagamore if I had been married in a church and had the reception elsewhere, but being married in the White House was really much the same thing. I was telling the truth when I was asked at Tricia Nixon's wedding whether it brought back any memories for me and I said, "Not a goddam thing." Despite all the publicity and brouhaha my wedding was a comparatively simple affair. As I remember it, at any rate. For weeks beforehand the press had been going on about my "trousseau" but there wasn't one as such. Just a few things I bought, including a depressingly muddy-colored going-away outfit, which I later regretted. But my wedding dress was quite pretty—white satin trimmed with lace from my mother's wedding dress and a really beautiful train of white and silver brocade. It had been especially woven, somewhere in New Jersey, I believe.

I'm told I fluctuated between animation and grimness on my wedding day. I remember coming down the stairs on the arm of my father, and all my brothers, with their hair plastered down, smirking at the bottom. I also remember the East Room, where the ceremony took place, being awash with flowers, mostly white, and thinking that it looked more like a funeral parlor and that I might swoon away from pure suggestion.

I wish more photographs had been taken of the ceremony. When one considers all the cameras there would be up and down the aisles at a White House wedding today, it's curious to think how very few pictures were taken in my day. Even those were done *very* discreetly. We had to climb up on a platform to help the focusing or something. The

With Nick Longworth and her father on her wedding day

The press at the wedding

Cuba's gift

Photo Fawcett.

CUBA'S GIFT TO MISS ROOSEVELT:
A 25,000-DOLLAR NECKLACE.

The necklet, which is of diamonds and pearls, was given partly in recognition of President Roosevelt's personal services during the war which liberated Cuba from Spain

Some of the guests

The decorations in the East Room

only funny incident I recall was when we—Nick, myself, and my father—were just about to be photographed in the Oval Room, and my veil had become disarranged and someone said, "Who is tall enough to adjust the bride's veil?" And up popped Franklin to do the job. I wish I had a picture of *that*. It shows what the times were like, though. Franklin was there but Eleanor was not. She couldn't go because that was indecent. She was having a baby (that was Anna about to be born). A pregnant woman at a wedding, going around *showing* herself! That just wouldn't do. Absolutely fantastic. So Franklin was there on his own.

The only other incident I remember was when I was leaving and saying good-bye to my stepmother. "Mother," I said, "this has been quite the nicest wedding I'll ever have. I've never had so much fun." And she, poor dear, obviously overexhausted by it all, said, "I want you to know that I'm glad to see you leave. You have never been anything but trouble." It was quite fantastic. It just came out like that. And I said, "That's all right, Mother. I'll be back in a few weeks and you won't feel the same way." And I was and she didn't. Well, I don't *think* she did. We were certainly able to laugh and jeer about a good many things together.

Years later, just before she died, she told me that she thought she had been very unkind to me when I was young. She hadn't really. In many respects she treated me better than she treated her own children. She appreciated her children when they were young, although she could be a tough disciplinarian; but it changed when they became older, except in the case of Kermit.

One thing I really relished about my wedding was the presents. Like everything else, they were exaggerated by the press but nevertheless they still gave greedy me a good deal of pleasure. When I was asked what I wanted as presents I said, "Trinkets, preferably *diamond* trinkets." I particularly liked the beautiful gold snuffbox from Edward VII with his miniature set in diamonds in the lid. I still have that. And then there was a beautiful Gobelin tapestry from the French government, a bracelet with diamonds (smaller than those he gave me when I christened his yacht, the *Meteor*) from the Kaiser, a rather hideous mosaic table from the King of Italy, and some really beautiful bolts of brocade from the Dowager Empress of China that kept me regally clad in the evening for decades.

Cuba sent me a superb string of pearls, thanks to Senator Lodge. Apparently the Cuban government had appropriated a certain sum and planned to give me a set of bedroom furniture inlaid with semi-precious stones. Senator Lodge told them, "I think Miss Alice would prefer a set of pearls." How right he was! So off they went to Boucheron in Paris and I was presented with this lovely thing, which I think I must have worn almost every day since. I'm sure I must have worn it at my wedding. I certainly put on everything I could find, including a number of things which probably weren't mine.

We went to Cuba for our honeymoon and we trod the old Rough Rider trail up San Juan Hill. The terrain was very different from what I had imagined. We were accompanied by a mule laden down with refreshments and I remember having a picnic by the side of the trail and being in a heated argument with Nick, about heaven knows what, under a tree.

One of the reasons I married was because I felt I had to get away from the White House and my family. I didn't want to stay there. I wanted a place of my own. I think I might well have gone abroad again if I hadn't married.

In any event my family *expected* me to be married. In those days the moment one had been "out" for two or three years one was expected to marry. If you didn't you ended up with a thermos of tea in your room, alone, like my poor Aunt Emily.

My father considered Nick Longworth a very good match. After all, he was Harvard and the Porcellian Club. My father said, "There's a young, new congressman coming in who might amuse you. He's Harvard and the Porc." He probably wouldn't have crossed my path otherwise. It was that bad.

There were—still are, as far as I know—two clubs at Harvard: the Porcellian and the A.D. Club, although members of the Porcellian never called it a club but a "society." My father took it very seriously. They all sang enormously patriotic songs—post-Civil War vintage— and drank each other under the table. Occasionally if you were married to one you were allowed near the place on certain occasions. It was the biggest snob thing you can possibly imagine. I think my brother Kermit got in. Archie did not. Nor, surprisingly, did Franklin, which I think caused a lasting wound. They used to call each other—rather facetiously but also rather seriously—"Brother" this and that. Brother Roosevelt and Brother Longworth. Oh dear!

My father wanted me to meet all kinds of people but not to marry them. A foreigner would have been bad, except perhaps an Englishman. A friend of Edith Wharton's would have been all right but not

Honeymooning in Cuba. (Right) The first quarrel

On San Juan Hill and going to Santiago. (Opposite). At the American Legation in Havana with the Minister (left) and Willard Straight

Mrs. Longworth, Sr., and Nick as a child with his sister, Clara. (Below) Rookwood, the Longworth home in Cincinnati

the Duke of Marlborough. He certainly didn't like the idea of poor Consuelo Vanderbilt being dragged weeping up the aisle by that great, dark, bristling mother of hers in order to marry him under duress.

He could be very pro-American in matters of that kind. It made him absolutely furious to know that the Duke of Abruzzi wasn't allowed to marry a nice American girl like Catherine Eakins. He was being painted by de Laszlo at the time this particular incident occurred and I only had to mention it—which I did on a number of occasions—for his amiable expression to turn into a frown immediately.

We used to accuse him of exaggerating his Americanism sometimes. Once when he was due to speak at the Guildhall we said, "Don't try and talk through your nose and say 'AMURIKA,'" so immediately he became terrifically, aggressively American and began talking in a kind of Middle West vernacular. There was a constant war between him and my stepmother over the pronunciation of words like tomato.

Nick was amusing. He didn't quite gobble books the way we did but he was a very talented musician, as were most of his family. There was something of an eighteenth-century parliamentary gentleman about him. One of his great-grandfathers had been the president of Harvard, and there were also Rieveses in his family, which was considered very good. There was lots of forelock pulling to the Rieveses, who were very grand Southern gentry.

Someone, someday should write a social history of families such as the Longworths of Cincinnati. They were the Magnificent Ambersons incarnate. They had come to Cincinnati in the late eighteenth century, crossed mountains with their lawbooks, and soon carved out small fortunes in real estate. Longfellow wrote about them in "The Queen of the West." Old Mr. Longworth imported vast amounts of Germans to do the vineyards he started there. He and the Astor of the time were reputed to be the richest men in America, but the vineyards (and a number of other enterprises) failed. The old ones planted the trees and their successors tried to keep them up. They were all frightfully place proud.

Rookwood, Nick's family home in Cincinnati, was *enchanting*, it was so awful. It was Hudson River Bracketed. The sort of thing Franklin's family had before they turned it into Long Island Georgian. Edith Wharton wrote about it in a very amusing way. It was built in the very worst Victorian tradition and was definitely out to impress. It was a series of brick boxes connected by a large "Italian style" brick tower. There was a large picture room full of rather dismal landscapes by early nineteenth-century Swedish painters. Nothing very good. At the bottom of the tower was the family bathroom, then there was another floor, then Nick's room, and at the top that insane, delightful man had a studio where he painted.

It was a very expensive house to run—it required a minimum of five servants—and I couldn't afford to keep it up when Nick died.

The Longworths were artistic, charming, and gifted but they had very little concern about their sources of income. The rents fell off, the taxes increased, and somehow they didn't seem to notice, with the result that there really wasn't very much money in the estate when old Mrs. Longworth died.

She was rather a formidable lady who was better dressed and straighter backed than anyone in Cincinnati. I see her now leaving the house in a carriage with a stream of little furs indecently assaulting each other round her neck and down her front. I enjoyed her in a way but I was never able to play the part of the dutiful daughter-in-law.

She spoiled her children and they spoiled her. They were a close family. There were two charming sisters, one of whom married Comte de Chambrun, whose family own Baccarat glass, which we all cheerfully began buying at a discount.

Nobody who didn't know Cincinnati life could describe it. It was a town with a great sense of its own importance. Not a common, vulgar, Midwestern town at all. You had arrived there either from the Western Reserve in the just post-colonial period or, even better, up from Virginia and Kentucky. They were all terribly nice and civilized. They traveled to Europe and promenaded along with the Anglais and they got presented at court and bought inferior pictures. They were very much that way. They considered Boston and Philadelphia to be all right, but New York was just a place one sailed to Europe from.

Nick's great-grandfather, Nicholas Longworth, had been one of the founders of the town. His son Joseph apparently spent most of his time reading, "collecting," and planting a good many trees at Rookwood. His artistic leanings seem to have been passed on to his children, but not any business sense.

There were a good many musical evenings at Rookwood—as often as three times a week. They used to be held in the so-called Picture Room and in the room next door there would be a table piled with sandwiches and drinks, where people could refresh themselves in the interval. Anyone caught starting a conversation during the music was

President and Mrs. Taft

shut up in the dining room. Once in a state of boredom bordering on stupefaction I said to the ardent music lover sitting next to me, "Isn't it extraordinary to think that Mozart never composed anything exclusively for the viola?" He looked perplexed for the rest of the evening.

Ohio politics could be fascinating. There was a large German and Dutch element in Cincinnati and it was curious how bigoted everyone was in those days about cultures other than the English. Then there were the bosses. George Cox and Mark Hanna were the two important ones. They were never invited to the house in Cincinnati. I don't think old Mrs. Longworth knew anything about bosses and things like that. I did, but that was different.

Taft was from Cincinnati. Dear Mr. Taft! I see him now, a great big pink porpoise of a man sitting in the back of an open touring car with his hands on his rotund belly. He was always very amiable to me. I think he had had to stand a lot in the corner when young, because he had a most dutiful streak, especially to Father. It was said he was a good hater, but I certainly never saw any of that. My father was devoted to him, although I don't think he thought he was a particularly good politician. I think my father would have been quite prepared to back someone like Elihu Root to succeed him, but the problem there was that Root was identified with interests, which made it impossible.

I think it would have been much better if Taft hadn't had the big-brother relationship with my father. He felt he had to keep on the same Cabinet and to continue the same policies of his predecessor and friend, which was wrong.

We always understood that Mrs. Taft took an enormous personal interest in what went on. She was a woman full of gentilities and she quickly became very possessive of the White House. She had the idea of having liveried men at the front door and things like that. And she took to driving in state around the Potomac to listen to the band. It might have worked in the era of carriages and landaus but with the advent of exhaust-spewing automobiles it only caused traffic jams and a lot of dazed-looking ladies clutching parasols and hats. I think her personality had a good deal to do with the breakup of Taft's friendship with my father. There was an abrasive quality there. The Longworths were particularly pleased with Taft's victory, much to my chagrin, and some cracks began to appear in my beautiful friendship with the family.

A few years before there had been an outcry from the Tafts when my father appointed Henry White as ambassador to Paris. Previously, when White had been secretary in London, he had, I imagine inadvertently, obtained tickets for the Tafts to visit the Royal Mews (stables) rather than the House of Commons and Mrs. Taft had been incensed at what she considered a monumental slight. It was all too silly.

When we left the White House just before Taft's inauguration we drove away and I was sitting in the front with the chauffeur. I had perfected what I called Mrs. Taft's hippopotamus face and was able to put it on just as we were going through the gates and say, "This, darlings, is what is coming after you."

I also buried a voodoo in the garden of the White House for good measure. Perhaps they will find it one day and say, "How strange!" Nobody likes to leave the White House, whatever they say. We were no exception. There is a photograph of the whole family about to leave and I must say we look as if we are being expelled from the Garden of Eden. There was a dinner the night before we left. I've forgotten who

Leaving the White House in 1909

exactly was there. Elihu Root, Mabel Boardman, Archie Butt, and a number of others. Mr. Root practically wept into his soup. He cried easily. Afterwards we went upstairs to that very pretty yellow Oval Room and suddenly I looked out of the window and shouted triumphantly, "It's snowing." That will take care of the inauguration, I thought. Next morning I went to see Father off. As soon as Taft was inaugurated he positively leapt for the train. It was still snowing.

Mabel Boardman, who was devoted to both the Tafts, was a great friend of mine. She had been on the Far East trip. We used to tease her about being in love with Mr. Taft, which was perfect nonsense. We used to say that she was going to be the Pompadour of the Taft administration. I can't tell you what a formidable creature she was to look at. Very tall and commanding. She later became the head of the Red Cross and looked every inch the part. "Now, Mabel," we used to say, "you are going to be a Power when Mr. Taft comes to office." I was devoted to her.

Archie Butt[29] was another good friend. Archibald Willingham Andrew Brackenbreed . . . *Butt*, we used to chant, teasing him about his name, which we said sounded like a load of coal falling downstairs. He had a very good sense of humor.

I went to Europe the first summer after my marriage. It was very tame in comparison to the Far East. Being presented at the court of the Dowager Empress was far more exciting than at the Court of St. James's, where I trotted out my wedding dress for the second time and wore the prescribed three ostrich feathers in my hair. There is an illustration from a contemporary issue of the San Francisco *Examiner* which shows an artist's rendering of the scene. There I am "bending the knee" and in a corner is a detailed diagram of just how this is done. If I had followed anything so complicated I would certainly have broken my neck. I have only the haziest recollection of the whole event. It couldn't have taken more than a few moments. One waited in an anteroom. I remember the closeness of the atmosphere, the slightly pervasive smell of nervous sweat and mothballs. Then one was announced, went in, curtsied, and went out. That was that. Couldn't have been simpler. The press made a tremendous thing of it, however, and also about the fact that Nick wore court breeches, which was considered to be kowtowing to English custom and not at all "Amurican." It all seems so silly that anyone even cared about anything so trivial even in those appearance-conscious days. But they did.

I had a chance to see more of Edward VII that summer. I sat next to him at a dinner party which the Reids (our ambassador in London) gave at Dorchester House, a most beautiful building on the site where the hotel is now. He couldn't have been more charming. Germanic but fun. Nothing difficult about him at all. The Duke of Marlborough sat on the other side at the same dinner. He was a bad little man, rather mean but amusing. He said, "Do you know Eleonora Sears?" and I said yes, and he said that she was someone who wanted to marry Harold Vanderbilt. He had obviously *ached* to marry a Vanderbilt too. Eleonora Sears was a fascinating woman. She was the first of the masculine young girls. A low voice and sensible shoes. That kind of thing. She couldn't have been more fun. Snarled a lot but with great wit.

I also met Queen Alexandra. She invited me to tea at Buckingham Palace. It was all very informal. Or relatively so. She was very deaf but it didn't seem to worry her much. She kept up a fluttery irrelevant conversation. She was still a very good-looking woman with a slim figure

A contemporary view of Alice's presentation at court

HOW MRS. ALICE ROOSEVELT LONGWORTH WILL MAKE HER BOW TO ROYALTY

How a Woman Must Make Her Curtsy When Presented to Royalty.

1. Attitude on Greeting Royalty.
2. The Beginning of the Curtsy.
3. The Lowest Point of the Curtsy. A, the left foot in the first position; B, sidewise movement of the foot to kick back the skirts; C, backward movement of the left foot, while the right knee is bent almost to the ground.

FIRST PICTURE AND DETAILED SKETCH OF THE GOWN THE PRESIDENT'S DAUGHTER WILL WEAR WHEN SHE IS PRESENTED AT COURT THIS MONTH

Racing on the Kaiser's yacht at Kiel. 1906

Eleonora Sears (right) and friend

In London. Summer 1906

Washington. 1912

To
my over-sized
surrogate
GRANDAUGHTER
ROBERT...
Alice Lee
ROOSEVELT
LONGWORTH-

With Manchu in 1910

and a charming well-poised little head. I felt very much at home with her because both in appearance and manner she reminded me very much of so many women I knew, who used her as their model.

Also that summer we went to Germany and sailed with the Kaiser at Kiel and he gave us an enormous dinner on board his yacht. He was a loquacious, rather restless person, but very friendly and interested in everything one had to say, even though he only listened to a fraction of the answers one gave to his many questions. Two of his sons, who had a house in Kiel, also gave us a party. Like so many royalties, they loved simple entertainments, not to mention simple humor, and we played tag and catch-as-catch-can on the tennis court.

Edwardian royalties seem to have been divided fairly between the major and the minor ones. It was amusing to see the veiled contempt with which they regarded each other. I remember after my father came back from the wake dinner following Edward VII's funeral he told us that he was talking to some unobjectionable but insignificant Balkan monarch when the Kaiser came up and said, "Don't bother about him, he's nothing. Now, here's a good fellow," and presented him to the King of Spain.

Americans held foreign royalty in some awe at that time. Look at Prince Henry's visit in my father's time. Then in the twenties we had Queen Marie of Rumania, who was very pleasant and English and enjoyable in private but who knew just how to act up in public, so that she became lionized as kind of a fairy-tale figure with her floating veils and long ropes of pearls. Pearls were very much part of regal uniform, especially of middle European queens. All those long drop pearl earrings with diamond studs. I think they must have worn them as an insignia of club membership.

Pearls were also very popular with the portrait painters of the period. They liked to portray them cascading down all those imposing white Edwardian bosoms. Poor old Auntie Bye had to drape herself in ropes and ropes of pearls for de Laszlo when he painted her. She didn't have enough of the real ones, so she had to get imitation ones just to get the effect he desired. At least toying with them allowed her to show off her really beautiful hands, which is perhaps why de Laszlo insisted she wear them in the first place.

One got one's first *jeune fille* pearls about the age of thirteen. They were usually small and modest. One graduated to slightly larger ones when one "came out" or got married.

To some it was considered important who one received jewelry from. I remember one afternoon rowing on the river at Farmington with Eleanor. For some reason or other she started lecturing me on the sort of presents one could receive from gentlemen—flowers, books, cards were all possible, I was assured, but jewelry of any kind, absolutely not. I listened to her earnest discourse, fingering all the while a modest string of seed pearls that an admirer had given me the week before.

Poor Eleanor! She took everything—most of all herself—so tremendously seriously. If only she had allowed a little levity into her life. She had a *miserable* childhood, which I don't think she ever got over. There was her exquisite, empty-headed mother, Anna Hall, who was one of the most beautiful women of her time. She was rather mean to Eleanor. She called her "Granny" and made her feel unwanted and unattractive. Eleanor also had two very pretty Hall aunts and a hateful grandmother. Then there was her father, my Uncle Ellie, who was the black sheep of the family.[30]

Someone should write something on Uncle Ellie and subtitle it "The Rake's Progress." There was this attractive and intelligent young man who ruined himself with drink. He was considered far more promising than my father when young but once he started hitting the bottle his slide downhill was spectacular. My father was always having to save him from some predicament. Conversation about Uncle Ellie and his problems was frequent when I was young. I could tell because it would stop when I entered the room. So I started listening at keyholes instead. That's how I learned of my father's departure for Europe to take Uncle Ellie out of the dives of Paris and the arms of a series of rather nice mistresses, who apparently were frightfully responsible about him.

Apparently he had a form of epilepsy which obviously wasn't helped by the drinking. I have only vague recollections of him, usually fast-moving ones. He would take one for walks as a child and would set off at such a pace that one's feet barely touched the ground.

He died when I was about ten and there was a lot of grief-making in the family. Auntie Corinne was particularly devoted to him. I am told there is a picture somewhere of Uncle Ellie laid out on his deathbed with Auntie Corinne grieving a good deal at the foot, two of his mistresses doing the same on either side and a large picture of his wife looking detached above the bedhead. Oh, how the Victorians

Eleanor Roosevelt's mother, Anna Hall

Eleanor in 1892

relished that sort of thing! The black sheep who finally succumbed. I was always intrigued by the strange contrast between the *louche* Uncle Ellie and that pillar of rectitude, my father.

Uncle Ellie's death must have had a dreadful effect on Eleanor. She had always doted on him and had been kept away from him. Much of her shyness and sense of insecurity stemmed from her enforced separation from him and the unhappiness it created. I understood that at a fairly early age. In a way we both suffered from being deprived of a parent. She had an idealized image of her father and I had one of my mother. But whereas she responded to her insecurity by being do-goody and virtuous I did by being boisterous and showing off. She got so little enjoyment out of things. If only she had dug in once in a while.

I suppose I was rather unpleasant as a child. Certainly I was pretty selfish and defiant from a very early age. Nobody spoiled me. I spoiled myself. I didn't do any of the nice and proper things expected of me. Whereas Eleanor certainly did. She always made a tremendous effort to do everything she thought was expected of her. She was always *so* good and *so* nice about everybody that it became quite intolerable, especially as one knew she harbored quite a lot of well-hidden resentments.

I saw a lot of her as a child, especially at Auntie Bye's. Helen Roosevelt, who was Franklin's half-niece, Eleanor, and I were fairly close as children. Helen was a little older than both of us and Eleanor was just under a year younger than I.

Many aspects of Eleanor's childhood were indeed very unhappy but she had a tendency, especially in later life, to make out that she was unattractive and rejected as a child, which just wasn't true. She claimed that nobody liked her. Well, *we* all liked her. She made a big thing about having long legs and having to wear short dresses. Well, as far as I was concerned, I envied her long legs and didn't notice her short skirts, if indeed they were short. She was always making herself out to be an ugly duckling but she was really rather attractive. Tall, rather coltish-looking, with masses of pale, gold hair rippling to below her waist, and really lovely blue eyes. It's true that her chin went in a bit, which wouldn't have been so noticeable if only her hateful grandmother had fixed her teeth. I think that Eleanor today would have been considered a beauty, not in the classical sense but as an attractive, rather unusual person in her own right.

I had a lot of admiration for her. But I did—still do—get bored with her type of piety. I can still see those large blue eyes fixed on one,

*T.R. (left) as a young man with his brother Elliott. 1880 (Right)
Eleanor Roosevelt aged seven wearing a mourning sash*

worrying about one, and wanting you to know that in her you had a friend. She always wanted to discuss things like whether contentment was better than happiness and whether they conflicted with one another. Things like that, which I didn't give a damn about.

She had one of those rather high, emphatic voices. So did Auntie Corinne. I didn't have it because I firmly kept away from it. It may have had something to do with that Southern grandmother but they tell me, no, it's the voice of well-brought-up little brownstone-front girls. I can imitate it pretty well and it is true that Eleanor asked me to do so at a party once in the White House and I was only too happy to oblige.

Some writer once stated that I was frightfully put out because Eleanor was so much more like my father than any of his own children. In some respects she probably was and indeed he was very fond of her. Certainly he had a do-gooding side to him too, which I suppose he got from *his* father. I'm all for it as long as I don't have to do it myself.

When Eleanor married Franklin I don't think it caused any particular excitement in the family. I was a bridesmaid at their wedding in New York. My father, who gave Eleanor away, lived up to his reputation of being the bride at every wedding and the corpse at every funeral and hogged the limelight unashamedly. I saw a photograph of Eleanor at her wedding the other day and thought it was a picture of me at mine. We looked so alike.

I think Franklin was very much in love with Eleanor when he married her. He had missed out on quite a few things when he was young. He confessed to a friend at Harvard when he wasn't elected to the Porcellian, "You never chose me for the best things." Despite Hyde Park and the money they didn't want him in the Porcellian. He was never quite on the top of certain things.

I liked Franklin rather more than the rest of the family did. One could always have fun with him. And he was great to tease. We used to call him "Feather Duster" (for Franklin Delano) because he pranced around and fluttered. He was rather hampered by being virtually an only child. He had one much older half brother and he had nieces and nephews who were younger than he was. He was overprotected by his formidable mother, Cousin Sally, who was a domineering tartar. Eleanor had a lot to put up with from her. She used to call her Mamá with the accent on that syllable. Cousin Sally had many dislikes and disapprovals. So did Eleanor although she disguised them better.

The Delanos were a fascinating family. Much more so than the Roosevelts. I was particularly interested in their trading connections with the Far East and was very impressed that Cousin Sally had actually sat on the knee of the famous Huqua in Canton. As a child, that is.

Franklin was said to be extremely attractive when he was young. We never considered him so. But then we were a large, rough, and boisterous family. Franklin used to sail a boat instead of sweatingly rowing it in the hottest weather as Father would insist on our doing. It was that kind of difference.

When Eleanor and Franklin first came to Washington they lived in a house on S Street. They would have rather fine and solemn little Sunday evenings where one was usually regaled with crown roast, very indifferent wine, and a good deal of knitting.

I remember going there once with my stepmother, who maintained that she could always tell when I was bored because I appeared to swell up. My eyes recede and my face becomes fat. My stepmother said she thought I was going to lose my eyes that evening. Both Eleanor and Franklin could be very boring together. But not when he was without her. Then he asserted himself.

Eleanor never took much interest in food—and certainly not in drink. Franklin had to sneak the occasional martini even when he was in the White House. But I suppose the riproaring example of Uncle Ellie would have been enough to turn anyone off drink for life. My stepmother shared Eleanor's aversion to a great extent and doubtless for the same reason. Except during Prohibition when she began serving the most extraordinary range of hideously colored cocktails at Sagamore. I don't think she knew what the word meant—let alone what went into them. She was just against Prohibition and being told what not to do.

I don't think Eleanor quite approved of my friendship with Franklin. I remember running into him once shortly after they were married. It was in the lobby of a hotel in Boston where I was staying overnight and I asked him up to my room for a drink. Actually it wasn't really my room. We just sat on a trunk in an alcove nearby and drummed our heels happily on it as we drank green mints and felt like leprechauns on a roof. Somehow Eleanor got to hear of it and was very annoyed and said to Franklin, "No one would know that you were her cousin. You were seen going to a woman's room. I think it would be a good idea if you and Alice didn't see each other for some time."

Lash in his excellent book on Eleanor and Franklin[31] puts forward the notion that perhaps I was interested in marrying Franklin and was put out when he chose Eleanor instead. Nothing could be further from the truth. I don't think it crossed either of our minds for a moment. I rather believe it was his cousin, Laura Delano, who first set that idea afoot.

Somebody has apparently broken the rather elementary code Franklin used in his Harvard diaries and had produced an entry which said in effect that he had "spent the evening with Alice, who confided in me, and worried over her all night." Well, I'm pretty certain it wasn't me. I would have known if it was. It was far more likely to have been Alice Parker, of whom he was very fond, much to Eleanor's chagrin.

Eleanor never could cope with Franklin's romantic affairs, especially not with Lucy Mercer, who was the most serious of them all. Lucy was beautiful, charming, and an absolutely delightful creature. I would see her out driving with Franklin and I would say things like, "I saw you out driving with someone very attractive indeed, Franklin. Your hands were on the wheel but your eyes were on her." And he would say, "Yes, she is lovely, isn't she?" and I would say, "Yes, she is indeed, Franklin."

I think their relationship was very much a lonely-boy-meets-girl thing. The rose behind the ear, the snipped-off lock of hair. That kind of thing.

Lucy was very attractive with a really lovely-shaped small head and she was always beautifully dressed. I don't really know how deeply involved she was with Franklin but Eleanor took the whole matter very seriously indeed and their relationship was never the same again. The Lucy Mercer thing really hurt her. She had always been uncertain and insecure about affection. My sister Ethel told me that she remembers Eleanor weeping on her shoulder when she was engaged to be married to Franklin and saying, "I shall never be able to hold him. He is so attractive." Poor Eleanor! It was all rather pathetic.

I remember Auntie Corinne telling me in that high, prim voice of hers, "Always remember, Alice, that Eleanor offered Franklin his freedom." Apparently there was a family conclave, presided over by Cousin Sally, and they talked over the whole matter of a divorce and they decided that there was Franklin with five children and Lucy, a Catholic, and they had better call it off. A year later she married Rutherfurd. When he died seven years later Franklin began seeing her again almost immediately. Eleanor was always furious about Lucy and never forgave Franklin his relationship with her.

I think Cousin Sally, who held Franklin's purse strings to a great extent, was instrumental in getting them to drop any idea of a divorce. She thought it would ruin his career. I don't think one can have any idea of how horrendous even the *idea* of divorce was in those days. I remember telling my family in 1912 that I wanted one and, although they didn't quite lock me up, they exercised considerable pressure to get me to reconsider. Told me to think it over very carefully indeed. The whole thing would have caused too much of a hullabaloo apparently. In those days people just didn't go around divorcing one another. Not done, they said. Emphatically.

So Eleanor was left with Franklin and look where it took her. Lash in his book says that when they (i.e. Eleanor and Franklin) came to the White House I was frightfully put out, which just wasn't true. I was furious, as I obviously would have been, by the fact that Franklin was being compared to my father. I was jealous about my father's position but not about my own. I'm surprised that Lash didn't realize this. I had this resentful feeling that my admired and respected parent was going to be forgotten with the new one coming up. But my father liked Franklin very much and he was very helpful to him. I wonder if Franklin would have emerged politically if my father had lived and had another term. Or indeed my father if McKinley hadn't been shot. To be honest, were it not for Mr. Leon Czolgosz we would probably have all been back in our brownstone-front houses and I would have doubtless married for money and been divorced for good cause.

We all wondered how Franklin would vote in the 1904 election—for his party or for his cousin. And he chose his cousin. We never returned the favor and none of our family ever voted for Franklin as far as I knew. We called him a maverick. We behaved terribly. There we were—*the* Roosevelts—hubris up to the eyebrows, *beyond* the eyebrows, and then who should come sailing down the river but Nemesis in the person of Franklin. We were out. Run over.

I really could have had a lot of fun with Franklin if only the damned old presidency hadn't come between us. There was this family feeling which I didn't brood about, but which was definitely there. It was complicated by the fact that my brother Ted had been brought up by my father to follow in his footsteps, which was very tough, and then to see Franklin follow in those same footsteps with large Democratic shoes on was just too terrible to contemplate! I could have had much more fun with Franklin if I hadn't had that feeling that it would be disloyal to my family.

My brother Ted campaigned against Franklin in 1920 and said that he was a maverick and had the brand of our family on him and Franklin, instead of saying, "I wear no man's brand," took it in the spirit it was meant (i.e. meanly) and got very annoyed and that was the beginning of very bad feeling. Then in 1924 when Ted ran for Governor of New York against Al Smith Eleanor started going around with a teapot strapped to the chassis of her car to imply that Ted had connections with the Teapot Dome scandal characters. And so the silliness went on.

Just after Franklin was elected Ted was asked what relation he was to the new President and he said, "Fifth cousin, about to be removed."[32]

After the Lucy Mercer affair, which hurt her very badly, and Franklin's illness, Eleanor came much more into her own. She developed a tougher side of her character, which was admirable even though it didn't bring much enjoyment to anyone, least of all herself.

She began to dress rather oddly and took to wearing some very bizarre-looking battered hats and bits of cat fur strung around her neck. She taught school for a while, went to Albany, and then she came out of it all and began to take a *real* interest in politics.

She always wanted to be somebody in her own right, not just as Franklin's wife. Corinne Alsop told me that after the election returns came in in 1932 Eleanor was found in a corner weeping and saying, "Now I will have no identity. I'll only be the wife of the President." Well, she quickly changed all that. And did a magnificent job into the bargain. She had high visibility and she worked tremendously hard. She always could talk, but she learned that good speechmaking was merely talking in public. She used the same phraseology as in conversation, without any affectation. Dame Rebecca West was rather funny once about Eleanor's tendency to treat this country as a giant slum area and it is true that she could be both a prig and a bore but that does not detract from some of her really remarkable achievements. She had an extraordinary career. Of all the Presidents' wives, none used her position in quite the same effective way that Eleanor did.

I only wish she had learned to enjoy herself a little more in doing so. She had so little enjoyment, so little amusement. She was so insecure about so many things.

I remember an evening once when Eleanor had returned early from a party, leaving Franklin to enjoy himself alone. After she had been dropped off at her house, she found she hadn't got her key with her. So what did she do? Call Franklin from a telephone booth? Go to the neighbors? Raise the servants? No, she lay down on the mat in the vestibule so that when Franklin came back in the small hours of the morning, all flushed with wine and good cheer, he was greeted by this wan apparition, looking like a string bean that had been raised in a cellar. "Why didn't you phone someone for help?" asked Franklin. "I've always understood one should try and be considerate of other people," she replied. I ask you! She could be quite maddening that way and she always seemed to manage to hold Franklin back from having a good time.

There was a more amusing side to her. She had a number of women friends, whom we used to allude roughly to as her "female impersonators." My cousin Helen had a horrible story—a delightful story —of being once in an adjoining room to one in which Eleanor and a couple of her female impersonators were having a pillow fight (apparently they used to leapfrog a lot as well). She had not had a very happy childhood, so of course it was nice for her to have some vigorous companions who adored her. Couldn't be better. More strength to all of them. Pillow fights were obviously as jolly a form of communication as any.

When Eleanor came to the White House she said to me, "You are always welcome here but you must never feel you *have* to come." So, far from feeling I had to go, I went with great alacrity and enthusiasm and had a lovely, malicious time. Then a little while later I had another communication from Eleanor. "I'm told you are bored at coming to the White House, and I never want you to be that, so . . ."

So I wrote her a very cheerful reply, saying, "How disagreeable people are, trying to make more trouble than there already is between us, and of course I *love* coming to the White House. It couldn't be more fun and I have always enjoyed myself immensely, etc., etc." Needless to say, she never asked me there again.

With Franklin it was always easier. We had a lot of laughs, but we also had some clashes.

I think, for instance, he resented the newspaper column I wrote, because in it I said some rather mean things about him. For example, I said—and this quite rightly made him hopping mad—that nobody should ever underestimate the way he behaved when he had infantile paralysis, and how he had managed to adjust himself to a permanently crippled condition. I maintained that, in the same way, he was trying to adjust this great lusty country into the same condition as his own. I suppose that was pretty nasty, but I happened to believe it was true at the time. We often forget that he was disabled. But he was, and there was never a recovery. Just bolstering up.

I remember on one occasion Franklin was on the point of signing some liquor bill, which was supposed to save the country a lot of money. I was at a reception at the White House and as I was leaving he said to me, "Do you know that after this is over I'm going upstairs and, by signing my name, I'm going to save the country fifty million dollars," and I said to him, "That's a drop in a bucket compared to what you are costing the country." He wasn't a bit amused by that. That's one of the troubles about the White House. It dulls. They just can't take things. Eleanor and Franklin shouldn't have minded my making merry of them. I've always laughed about all the family, including myself. I'm a comic character too.

Then in the war he talked scathingly about "these people on Massachusetts Avenue with twenty-room houses, who should turn them over to fill them."

I said, "Just how did Franklin get in and count the rooms in this house?"

I had great fun with Franklin in the First World War. One day Colonel Marlborough Churchill . . . odd name . . . who was head of G-2, which I think was the army Secret Service or something, came with an aide and said, "Mrs. Longworth, you have a chance to serve your country." At that time I was being criticized for *not* serving my country. I mean, I dished out ice cream to soldiers coming through and things like that, but nothing very serious. Neither was Colonel Churchill's offer, as I was soon to find out, when I discovered that all I was being asked to do was to look over transoms and peep through keyholes. Could anything be more delightful than that?

There was a certain lady, a young woman, very attractive and a friend of all of ours. She had taken a house with a big studio attached to it, and my G-2 colleagues said they were going to . . . what they now call . . . bug it. What they did was to put in hearing devices and they wanted me to go down and say where to put them. So I went and looked and told them that there was an upper balcony with a large swinging . . . well, not exactly a hammock but a kind of mattress on a swing. I thought that might be a good place for one of the devices, so they put one there and connected it to the studio. And then I and three or four absolutely charming and practically *invisible* Secret Service men went over there and heard the most enchanting conversation between this lady and my old friend Bernie Baruch.

A friend of mine, who was staying with the lady concerned at the time, had to leave documents around about such things as where the navy was going to be sent and things like that. They were false of course and were provided by Franklin. Apparently this lady had an uncle in Bucharest who handled her estate and he was supposed to be getting information from her from the false papers and people like Bernie Baruch, who knew everything.

We did hear her ask Bernie how many locomotives were being sent to Rumania, or something like that. In between the sounds of kissing so to speak. "You are a coward, you don't dare to look," was one of her lines.

Of course we were doing a *most* disgraceful thing in the name of looking after the affairs of our country, but it was sheer rapture!

Eleanor apparently knew about what was going on—as a great many people did—and years afterwards when Franklin was at the White House, we were both chuckling about the incident one time and Eleanor said, "You know, Alice, I have always disapproved of what you and Franklin were doing." Oh, we had such a hilarious time! He really could be the greatest fun.

I think Bernie enjoyed the whole thing too. Once much later he said that he had heard I was involved in the matter and I said, "Yes, I was, and all I can tell you is I hope you got what you wanted."

TIME

The Weekly Newsmagazine

ALICE ROOSEVELT LONGWORTH

Later Years

One of the great changes I notice in the political scene is the effect television has had. For instance there don't seem as many flamboyant figures and great speakers around as there used to be. They seem to be more uniformly packaged these days. And I don't think they debate nearly as much as they did. I remember when someone good was going to make an important speech, everyone *flocked* to the Congressional galleries. Now they say what they have to say on television.

I used to go to the debates a lot, especially during the early days of the League of Nations.

We were against the League because we hated Wilson, who was a Family Horror. He couldn't do any good in our eyes because he had beaten Father. We felt that my father had advocated the idea of the League of Nations in his Nobel prize acceptance speech. And then Taft had come up with his League to Enforce Peace and we had squabbled about that. We didn't like other people's Leagues muscling in on our own. It was entirely personal politics designed purely to annoy. As far as I was concerned anyway. All that nonsense about my killing the League with a bunch of diehard cronies is ridiculous. It is true that I took a great interest in the debates but I don't think I influenced matters one way or another. Wilson could have had his League any time. All he had to do was to take the reservations. But he had a slowness which verged on stupidity. We were not irreconcilable but we were against the League *in that form.*

Wilson was probably rather an interesting man but we had to put on a show of hating him. There was a sanctimonious quality about him which was frightfully annoying. Cabot Lodge scorned him because he wasn't really an intellectual like the Boston intellectuals. Then there was this image of the wonderful man who was saving the world, and we all made fun of *that.* We made bawdy jokes about him and the vari-

With her daughter Paulina in 1926

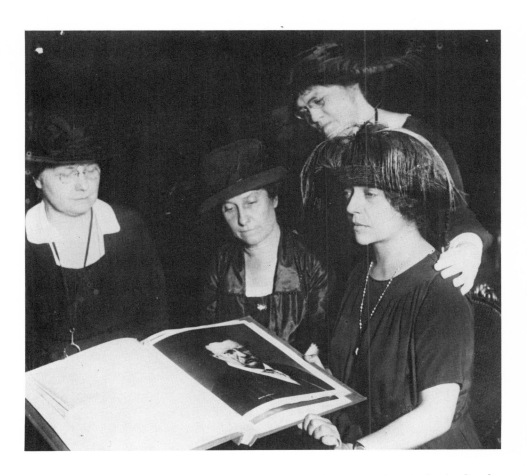

Mourning at the GOP Headquarters in 1919, just after her father's death

ous lady friends who *worshiped* him. Horrible man, we all said, chasing after women and then saying his prayers before leaping into bed with them. All *that* sort of thing.

When he had a stroke we heard he had grown a beard and we wondered whether he kept it outside or hidden under the sheets. He was only seen in bed by his Cabinet and toward the end not even by them, as his wife, quite rightly, kept everyone away.

Mrs. Wilson was a formidable-looking woman. She was given to wearing huge carnivorous-looking orchid corsages in the evening. We used to say that after dinner she would go upstairs, eat her orchids, and go to bed.

I can't remember going to the White House when Wilson was

Wearing trousers in Chicago. 1915

there. Oh yes, I did go once, to an "entertainment," but he was ill and never appeared, so Goethals[33] and I sat on little gold chairs in a corner and sneered and jeered about everything and had a wonderful time.

I had a personal grudge against Harding. At the 1912 convention he had worked actively against my father and then told Nick he could have "anything he wanted." I told him Nick wouldn't take anything from thieves and the feud was on. I didn't go to their home afterwards, although I did go a couple of times when he was in the White House. He was a very dull man. He was given to calling his girl friends "girlie" and he put the White House closets to a whole new range of uses. His wife was rather archly known as the Duchess, presumably after the one in *Alice in Wonderland* rather than any grandeur on her part. "Duchess," they would say as they played poker, "you are lying down on your job," referring apparently to her ability to get the drinks. She used to have a little red book in which she recorded the names of those who hadn't been civil to her since coming to Washington.

She asked me upstairs at the White House and in what had been my father's (and other Presidents') library I was shown every known gambling device and drinks galore—it was during Prohibition—and a general atmosphere of a convivial gambling saloon.

Coolidge by contrast was a precise little man. I didn't invent the phrase about him looking as if he had been weaned on a pickle but I certainly gave it currency. He did look just like that.

I went to a prize fight with him once. It was between Carpentier and Dempsey and we went by a special train, playing poker all the way. There was only one slight hitch. Mrs. Coolidge kept on calling me Alice and I was in the embarrassing position of not being able to call her by her first name because I didn't know it and didn't feel I could very well ask her husband what it was.

Coolidge could be taciturn to a degree. He came to dinner with us just before he left the presidency. Nick was the Speaker and, when he toasted the President, Coolidge said absolutely nothing. Just sat there. So finally Mrs. Coolidge got up and said a few words about how much they had enjoyed Washington. I was so furious I never said another word to him the rest of the evening.

I rather liked Hoover, especially in retrospect. Ogden Mills once told me that he had one of the best brains he knew. But he also had that stiff-collar quality, which was most unfortunate. I took Paulina down to see the Hoovers off the day before Franklin was inaugurated. There they sat like waxworks, all stiff, bruised, and wounded in the Green Room.

The next day I went to see him off at the station. There were lots of people there but they weren't especially friends of his. Franklin's inaugural address was being broadcast and just as soon as it was finished Hoover appeared and caught the train. He didn't wave. He didn't look around. There was no expression. He looked like a rather disappointed tortoise.

That night all was a riot of pleasure at Franklin's first official dinner in the White House. Triumph following a tremendous defeat. The contrast was extraordinary.

Washington was tremendously protocol-conscious in those days. Still is to a great extent. It was absolute agony to sit next to the same person night after night at dinner. I was landed with a particularly boring ambassador for the longest possible stretch. He was one of those joke diplomats with a monacle and a long, hatchet face and I had to sit next to him for what seemed like an eternity. Finally I begged one hostess to change the seating plan to allow me to get away and she promised she would but when the time came protocol won out and she lost her nerve and I was stuck with my bundle of fun once again.

Then there was all that brouhaha over Dolly Gann. She was the sister of Charlie Curtis,[34] who was then Vice-President, and there was a lot of speculation as to whether she should be considered his official hostess, as he had no wife. Eugene Meyer[35] was having a dinner where, according to custom, there would be lots to eat but nothing to drink. He said he was going to put Dolly Gann on his right and the British ambassadress on his left. When Nick learned this he said he wouldn't go to the dinner, citing the fact that Dolly Gann was being placed ahead of the British ambassadress but more pertinently because he didn't want to go to a "dry" dinner. The press built it up into one of those big things and there was a positive rustle in the press gallery like autumn leaves when I came into the visitors' gallery in the Senate together with Dolly Gann a few days later. There never was a feud between us despite the attempts to manufacture one.

Eugene Meyer had great charm. And a very dry wit. He once turned to me as I was sounding off on some subject I was not particularly well versed in and said, "You know, you say things with more finality to less foundation than anyone I know." I absolutely howled with pleasure.

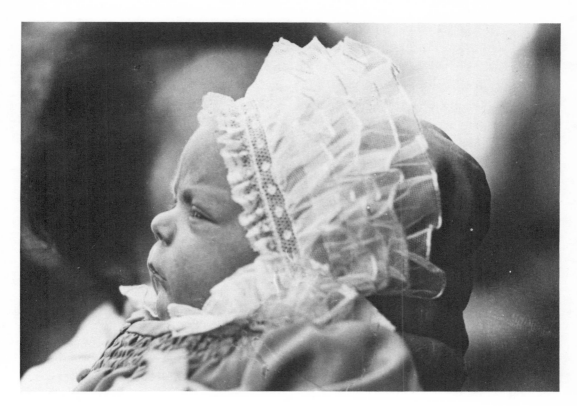

With Paulina, born in February 1925

There were a number of well-known hostesses when I came to Washington, although they weren't called hostesses. They were called heaven knows what. I remember one called Mrs. Hobson, who was known affectionately as the "Hobnob." She was amused and amusing and gave little Thursday evenings. She had a circle rather like Daisy Harriman used to.

Then there was Frances Wolcott, the wife of the senator from Colorado, who collared lots of Interesting People and had current events sessions for people who were Going Somewhere. We laughed a little about all that and said what a good job Mrs. Wolcott was doing to shed enlightenment in our nation's capital.

Daisy Harriman had by far the best salon. She was a fascinating, delightful creature. She began taking an interest in politics in Wilson's time and her parties, although there was quite a lot of tapping of spoons on glasses and "Now we are going to talk about . . ." were absolutely delightful. Everyone shone there. Her husband was dashing and good-looking. He was rich one week, poor the next. Unfortunately he died in one of his poor periods so Daisy wasn't particularly well off, but she bought this old boardinghouse near the F Street Club. It had a very pleasant garden and she held her parties there. She was one of those people who always manage to survive with great flair.

Washington went through a period of Great Revels in the twenties. For instance, they didn't have a ball when Harding was inaugurated because there was a great outcry about the expense, so there was a mass of private parties instead. Evalyn Walsh gave one of great grandeur in that extraordinary house of hers, which is now the Indonesian Embassy. I was always enchanted by it, it was so endearing in its vulgarity. And she could be very likable with her queer loud voice and great generosity.

A great friend of mine, Cissy Patterson, who owned the McCormick paper here, was another great party giver. She used to say that Evalyn Walsh's parties were the sort given by Moscow millionaires— before the Revolution presumably. You know, a hundred per table. That sort of thing. I sat once between Arthur Balfour and Bill Borah[36] at one of these byzantine revels and Balfour said that he felt like an orphan in a storm as the hordes whirled around us. Cissy was an enchanting creature. She had a tall, slim figure, great elegance of line, masses of red hair, brown eyes set very far apart, and a foolish little

The Massachusetts Avenue house, purchased in 1925

nose. Everybody said, "How charming she is despite her looks." Well, today she would doubtless be called a beauty. She wasn't by the standards of the time anyway. But she had an attraction and charm and vitality, which was much more important.

The other night at dinner there were two people who I call really great beauties. Evangeline Bruce and Fifi Fell. They both have the height, the slimness, that *raffiné* quality which, to me anyway, is the essence of beauty.

Grace Vanderbilt used to hold rather elaborate parties, especially at Newport. I remember a fancy dress ball which had the most intricate sets of quadrilles with the dancers in different costumes—Persian, Russian, Hussar, gypsies, and so on. We sat giggling from divans around the walls.

It was there that I first met F. E. Smith,[37] Churchill's great friend. My room had been turned into a cloakroom and I was at the dressing table when suddenly this apparition appeared, wearing a very fine Chinese robe, picked up my powder puff, and proceeded to powder his nose with great concentration. Later that evening he gave a toast to the "intoxicating women and the intoxicated men of Newport," which caused a buzz of consternation and a lot of angry, raised eyebrows (male).

Town Topics, which was a kind of scandal sheet when I was young, was supposed to be read avidly only belowstairs, but upstairs took pretty long peeks at it as well. It was considered absolutely horrifying in those days to have *printed* gossip. There was a columnist called Madame Devereux who, together with her daughter, Marion, produced a society column which was required reading if one enjoyed bizarre English. They would write about things like "The Flotsam and Jetsam of the Well-appointed Drawing Room." It was hilarious.

There was a tremendous amount of heavy drinking during Prohibition. Nineteen twenty was a particularly active year for drunks in my life. It was shortly before Harding was elected. There was a charming senator from Pennsylvania who had been a great friend of my father and whom I admired enormously. He was my dark horse. I met him once on the little tramway which runs between the Senate Office Building and the Capitol. He was as tight as a tick. Standing nearby was a senator from the driest part of the Midwest and I didn't want my dark horse to be seen in that condition so I lured him over to a corner where there was a large spittoon and suddenly he collapsed into it and squatted there like a character from *Alice in Wonderland*. I thought,

Voting in 1968

The sign in the image reads:

DISTRICT OF COLU[MBIA]
REGISTRATION
AND VOTING PL[ACE]
14
REGISTER H[ERE]
JAN F[...]
[...]DAYS 5-9PM 26
[...]URDAY 9AM-9PM 27
[...]TIONAL DATE TO BE ANNO[UNCED]
[V]OTE HE[RE]
[...] PRIMARY
PRESIDENTIAL ELECTION TUES[...]
[...]:00 AM - 8:00 P[M]

"My God, my dark horse has had a stroke." I leant forward to pull him up, but not realizing how light he was (or how strong I was), the next thing I knew he had landed on my shoulders and we stood there swaying like two derelicts until luckily my old friend Medill McCormick[38] appeared and pried my burden away. An hour or so later he was on the floor of the Senate smoking a big black cigar and appearing none the worse for wear.

Another friend who had frequent bouts with the bottle was that wonderful character Frank Brandegee, who was the senator from Connecticut. I used to offer him asylum in my house when things got too bad for him. He once spent ten days with me, sobering up in a back room. Cabot Lodge was very gloomy about the whole business and thought I was hiding the good senator so that he couldn't vote for the Four-Power Treaty. Dear Frank Brandegee. I can hear his high, slightly cracked New England voice now. We were driving around Washington late at night once in my small "electric" and he suddenly laughed about something and I said, "How nice to hear you laugh," and he said, "That's not laughter, my dear, that's the hysteria of despair." He was absolutely enchanting.

I had a butler about this time who was also given to drink. I didn't realize it, however, until one day he appeared at the head of the stairs dressed in a most elegant Charvet dressing gown and carrying a pail of water in one hand. There was a very large water mark on the wall nearby. "What's that?" I asked. "A large strange-looking cat was coming up the stairs, so I threw some water at it," he said. The following day he had to be admitted to a "home" suffering from a bad case of *delirium tremens*.

There were a number of really able members of the Senate in the twenties, Jim Reed, Oscar Underwood, John Sharp Williams,[39] and Bill Borah among them. Jim Reed was a fantastic orator with a saturnine voice. We were driving around near Wilson's house the night after he died and there were a lot of people there weeping and on their knees. "Like fleas who have lost their dog," he said with his distinctive snarl.

Borah was a great friend. Like Reed, he was a great speaker. He had never been abroad. He had nearly drowned as a child apparently and he was afraid of crossing water. He came from a remote area of Illinois known as Little Egypt because of its flat delta land. He had a great leonine head and was a fascinating conversationalist. He could hold one spellbound for hours with tales of labor disputes in Illinois at the turn of

With the Johnsons

And the Eisenhowers

With President and Mrs. Kennedy

And Bobby Kennedy

With Joanna in Wyoming

In Hong Kong

And at home, 1976

Putting on Mrs. Taft's "hippopotamus face"

And Eleanor Roosevelt's toothy grin

Having a conversation with Cat

the century. Unusual subjects like that. But there was a withdrawn, rather secretive quality about him, which seemed to hold him back. He was a most intriguing person.

Both John Lewis, who was another close friend, and Borah were remarkably similar in looks and also, to some extent, in temperament. They had the same large, shaggy heads and they both alternated between being very stimulating or very taciturn. They were *never* boring. Humor was the great bond between us.

Someone should do a study on charm in politics. People like my father, like Franklin, like Jack Kennedy were very engaging to begin with. When you add to that the glamor attached just to being in the White House, they become almost irresistible. The particular charm of the Kennedys was that they had a good deal of fun and often had their tongues in their cheeks at the same time. The Nixons didn't.

The Kennedys reminded me of all those Irish who came over in the 1840s. They seemed to have a rather special quality. There were all these marvelous-looking kitchen maids and policemen, who might eas-

Reading at home. 1978

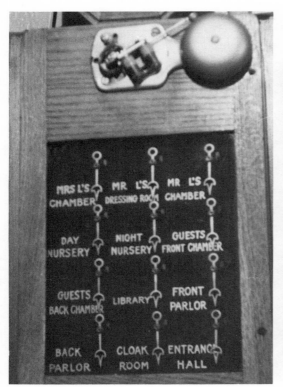

The call indicator in the pantry

Dinner going up in the dumbwaiter

Janie in the pantry

And in the kitchen

The table set for a dinner party

The living room

In the Collyer room

With Cat

The hats in the closet

The Holy Family of the GOP

ALL   THIS

AND
TRUMAN,
TOO.

Batchelor's cartoon

Sargent's water color of the White House

ily be Sargent Shriver. I'm not being snobbish. It's just that rare quality which the Irish and no other nation seem to have. I never had much time for old Joe Kennedy but I've always thought Rose Kennedy is an extraordinary woman and it was fun to see her delightful offspring enjoying themselves.

The Kennedys were a fascinating, incredible outfit. There hasn't been anything like them since the Bonapartes. I had great fun with them, especially Jack. He loved to tease and he could be very amusing. He also had a *real* feeling for learning. Both he and Bobby were eager to supplement their education by learning more. They really wanted to know.

Bobby was much the more serious of the two. He was a priest *manqué*. I used to tease him a lot and he couldn't take a good deal of it. For instance, there was a time when he had just climbed a mountain in Canada and his brother Teddy said that he had climbed an even higher one there and hadn't needed the help of the Canadian Mounted Police. Well, I reminded Bobby of *that* and went on to quote something from Longfellow:

> A youth who bore, through snow and ice,
> The banner with a strange device,
> Excelsior!

I told him that I had heard he had carried a banner with the very strange device of three leprechauns, and that made him even more furious. He could give as good as he got and we goaded each other with obvious relish for a number of years.

Jackie is someone I can always laugh with. It's fascinating to see how that golliwog of a girl developed into such an enchanting creature. She really bloomed, especially when she was in the White House. Now she looks like a figure out of a Minoan frieze.

Eisenhower was a pleasantly avuncular figure, ideal, I suppose, for the times, but there were certainly no sparks there. It was rather amusing to see how Mamie was held up as this Exhibition Mother-in-law thing, in Nixon's time, when you think how Eisenhower did his best to dump Dick Nixon when he was Vice-President! At the time we all said, "Don't let him dump you." We were really pushing him to stand firm and not to be taken off the ticket.

With Queen Elizabeth II at the White House. July 1976

President Nixon talking to guests at her ninetieth birthday party in 1974.
Her dressmaker, Madame Fagasta, on the right

Somebody once calculated that I had been to an average of 2.7 dinners a year at the White House over a sixty-year period. That's an awful lot of dinner. There was a certain similarity about them—the attentive aides, the Marine band, etc. And I never liked it when they started braying your name out over a loudspeaker. A friend of mine, who disliked this practice as much as I did, threatened to do something about it. I had visions of her whipping out a pistol and shooting the offending speakers into silence. And the trouble about having loudspeakers to call up one's car is that one can't slip away early without being noticed.

The Nixons had a tendency to mix the most rabid warmongers with the gentlest doves at some of their parties during the Vietnam War. The result was not always as interesting as it might have been.

I seem to have known the Nixons ever since they came to Washington in the late forties. There was always a stubborn persistent quality about him which some people admired and others couldn't stand. They *minded* him so, even long before Watergate. A lot of hatred focused on him in much the same way as it had done on McCarthy. Now *there* was a cheap creature. He had the easy manners of a perfect jay. I remember him once coming up to me at a party, putting his arm

Cradling her foot

With Joanna, 1978

around my shoulder, and saying with a kind of yokel jocularity, "Ah, here is my blind date. I'm going to call you Alice," and I said, "No, Senator McCarthy, you are *not* going to call me Alice. The truckman, the trashman, and the policeman on the block may call me Alice but you may not." I never saw him again after that.

I was rather fond of the Johnsons. Lyndon was an engaging rogue elephant of a man. He used to complain that he couldn't kiss me under my hat and I told him that was why I wore it.

I've had a lot of fun in Washington. I enjoy my house. I'm amused by the fact that when I first came here over fifty years ago I was told it was far too small to entertain properly in. Now it is called a "mansion" (horrid word) and shown to tourists as some kind of dodo's antediluvian lair. Anyway, whatever it is called, it is shabby and comfortable and I like it. I also like being close to Dupont Circle with its hippies and pushers and banners saying things like "Three Cheers for Jesus."

Most of my old tribal friends are either dead or barely tottering over the Hindu Kush with a Smithsonian tour and here am I, like the character in the ballad:

> I'm growing deaf,
> My lungs are far from strong.
> I stoop and shuffle like a chimpanzee,
> My stories are interminably long.
> I laugh at them myself consummately.
> I talk about my mother's pedigree,
> I note a tendency to avarice.
> These are thy wages, O debauchery,
> What is the use of going on like this?

When I look back from my vantage point of advanced age, I can see why I made Washington my home. I think I would have found anything else rather dull in comparison. But Washington is a small, cozy town, global in scope. It suits me. And having graduated from being considered rather a loathsome combination of Marie Dressler and Phyllis Diller, I seem to have achieved a symbolism of sorts in my dotage. Rather like Queen Victoria, I fear, but hopefully with more levity. All I've really done is to have a good time. I've covered a lot of territory. I'm amused and, I hope, amusing. I've always believed in the adage that the secret of eternal youth is arrested development.

Notes

1. *Before the Colors Fade*, by June Bingham. American Heritage. Feb. 1969.
2. Earl Grey's tea was the name given to the blend by the 2nd Earl Grey in 1830. Only Jackson's of Piccadilly had the original recipe. Mrs. Longworth had drunk this particular blend since childhood, so when Jackson's closed in 1978 there was some concern about keeping her adequately supplied.
3. *Cookbook of the Performing Artists of the Kennedy Center.*
4. *Captain Craig*, by Edwin Arlington Robinson.
5. *Cautionary Verses*, by Hilaire Belloc.
6. *The Jungle Book*, by Rudyard Kipling.
7. *Urne-Buriall V*, by Sir Thomas Browne.
8. Theodore Roosevelt, Sr. (1831–78), father of President Theodore Roosevelt. His brother who lived next door on Fifty-seventh Street was James Alfred Roosevelt (1825–98).
9. Martha Bulloch Roosevelt (1825–84).
10. Anna Bulloch Gracie was the sister of Martha Bulloch Roosevelt and had lived with the family and helped with the children's education for a number of years before marrying James Gracie.
11. George Cabot Lee and Caroline Haskell Lee.
12. Anna Roosevelt (1853–1931). "Auntie Bye" was the elder sister of Theodore Roosevelt. She became Mrs. William Sheffield Cowles.
13. Isabella Selmes (1886–1953) was married first to Robert Ferguson then to Jack Greenway. Both men had been well-known Rough Riders.
14. Edith Carow (1861–1948) married Theodore Roosevelt as his second wife in December 1886.
15. Gertrude Carow (1835–95) married Charles Carow and was the mother of Edith Carow Roosevelt.
16. Sir Cecil Spring-Rice (1859–1918). Secretary at the British Legation in Washington 1887–95. Ambassador 1913–18.
17. Corinne Roosevelt (1861–1933), younger sister of Theodore Roosevelt. She married Douglas Robinson.
18. The children of Theodore and Edith Roosevelt were:

Theodore	(1887–1944)
Kermit	(1889–1943)
Ethel	(1891–1977)
Archibald	(1894–1979)
Quentin	(1897–1918)

19. George Borrow, author of *The Romany Rye*.
20. Thomas C. Platt (1833–1910), Senator from New York.
21. Emily Carow (1865–1939), younger sister of Edith Roosevelt.

22. Written in 1902 to Mrs. Bessie Van Horst and published as a preface in the book *The Woman Who Toils*.

23. Both Mabel Boardman, later the head of the Red Cross, and Mrs. Newlands, wife of the Senator from Nevada, were in the party.

24. Willard Straight (1880–1918). Married Dorothy Whitney.

25. Gifford Pinchot (1865–1946), Chief Forester in Theodore Roosevelt's Administration.

26. Elihu Root (1845–1937). Secretary of State in Theodore Roosevelt's Cabinet.
    Philander Knox (1853–1921). Attorney-General in the cabinets of both McKinley and Theodore Roosevelt.
    John Hay (1838–1905). Secretary of State, 1898–1905.
    Henry Cabot Lodge, Sr. (1850–1924). Senator from Massachusetts.

27. Jennie Jerome (1854–1921), the American-born mother of Winston Churchill.

28. Bourke Cockran (1854–1923). Congressman and distinguished orator.

29. Archibald Butt (1865–1912). Military aide to Presidents Theodore Roosevelt and Howard Taft. Died on the *Titanic*.

30. Elliott Roosevelt (1860–1894), younger brother of Theodore Roosevelt. Married Anna Hall and was the father of Eleanor Roosevelt.

31. *Eleanor and Franklin*, by Joseph Lash.

32. In 1932–33 Theodore Roosevelt, Jr., was Governor-General of the Philippines appointed by Hoover. His relationship to Franklin Roosevelt was fifth cousin once removed, so his remark was both clever and accurate. He was replaced.

33. General George Washington Goethals (1858–1928). Chief engineer of the Panama Canal.

34. Charles Curtis (1860–1936). Senator from Kansas and Vice-President under Hoover.

35. Eugene Meyer (1875–1959), the newspaper executive, owner of the Washington *Post*.

36. William Edgar Borah (1865–1940). Senator from Idaho.

37. Frederick Edwin Smith, later Earl of Birkenhead.

38. Medill McCormick (1877–1925). Senator from Illinois. Married Ruth Hanna, who was a very good friend of Mrs. Longworth.

39. James Alexander Reed (1861–1944). Senator from Missouri.
    Oscar Wilder Underwood (1862–1929). Senator from Alabama.
    John Sharp Williams (1854–1932). Senator from Mississippi.